The Ultimate Guide
Wallpaper

Charlotte Abrahams

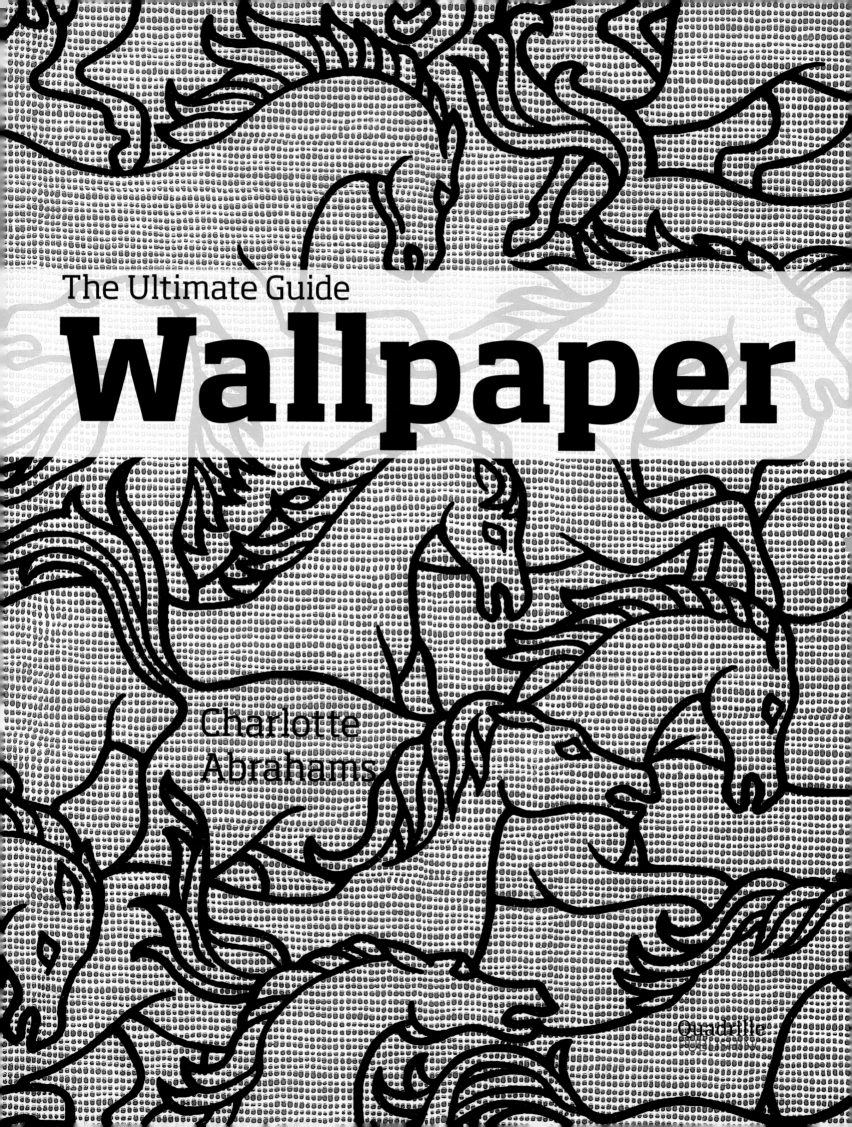

The Ultimate Guide

Wallpaper

Charlotte Abrahams

Quadrille
PUBLISHING

For George, Hamish and Paddy,
with love and thanks.

Contents

Introduction

Wallpaper is back at the forefront of interior fashion but its story is one of fluctuating fortunes. Ten years ago, 80 years ago, 140 years ago, papered walls were beyond passé; today, as in the eighteenth century, they are the last word in decorative chic. All fashions are cyclical of course, but wallpaper's continual resurgence can be put down to two things: technological innovations and – more importantly – our innate desire to decorate the walls which surround us.

The invention of wallpaper was not a single eureka moment but rather a halting evolution, subject to a myriad of outside influences, including the imposition of taxes and the outbreak of wars which closed trading routes and halted production.

Its beginnings are vague; inextricably bound up with the emergence of a proper paper industry (wallpaper couldn't exist until there was a steady supply of good quality paper on which to print it) and the development of wood block-printing techniques, but it is generally accepted that by the sixteenth century paper had become a widely used decorating device. (Britain's oldest known wallpaper dates back to around 1509. A formalised pomegranate design inspired by Italian damask, it was discovered in 1911 on the ceiling of rooms in the Master's Lodge at Christ's College, Cambridge.)

The early papers were printed on individual sheets of waste paper (condemned literature was a common source) measuring around 30cm x 36cm, which was the same size as the sieves used in the paper manufacturing process. The designs, rough imitations of popular textiles, were printed in black and white using wood blocks and carbon ink and the finished papers – or Dominos as they were known – were most often used to line chests and boxes. When they were used on walls, they were first pasted onto a canvas backing and then nailed to the wall in the same way as traditional fabric hangings.

On small sheets, paper, however beautiful, was impractical as a wallcovering. To have any hope of survival the Dominos had to be joined together. Continuous rolls appeared for the first time in the seventeenth century. Consisting of 12 joined sheets, these new rolls were around 10.5 metres long – which is still the standard roll length today. The move from sheets to rolls had an enormous effect and by the last quarter of the century wallpaper had established itself as an economically viable alternative to tapestries and textile hangings.

Its chief consumer was the emerging merchant class. These people needed aesthetically pleasing, reasonably priced materials with which to decorate their newly built homes and wallpaper fitted the bill perfectly. Designed to resemble the fine tapestries and intricate wood panels found in the grand houses of Europe, wallpaper enabled the bourgeoisie to get the aristocratic look they aspired to without the financial outlay.

The next major development occurred at the start of the eighteenth century. Until this time, wallpaper had been formed into rolls after printing, which meant that pattern repeats could be no larger than the old Domino sheets. Now, thanks to technological advances, the process was reversed and designers were suddenly presented with a canvas 12 times the size. Large-scale repeats had arrived.

These imposing designs marked a shift in the public's perception of wallpaper. No longer simply wannabe fabric, wood or marble for people too impecunious to have the real thing, it began to be seen as a desirable product in its own right – and therefore something the rich should own. (For most of the previous century, the seriously wealthy considered wallpaper to be fit for only the servants' rooms.) In Britain, which dominated the market until the 1770s, demand rose to such an extent that, in 1712, Queen Anne declared wallpapers a luxury item and imposed a tax accordingly. Exports however were exempt – a fact that helps to explain the rapid, international spread of British wallpapers.

But while the British industry was certainly flourishing (by 1800 there were around 150 paper stainers in the country) it was not unrivalled. Trade with the Far East prompted a craze for all things Oriental, including extravagant and highly coloured 'China Papers' produced specifically for export to Europe, while the French put all their efforts into quality. 'Manufacturer Royale', Jean Baptiste Reveillon, for example, specialised in colourful, block-printed papers featuring classical motifs such as urns, flowers and birds designed to be hung as panels in the homes of the French aristocracy. America didn't have a wallpaper industry of its own at this time (the first wallpaper factory opened in 1765), but they imported the stuff with a passion and, in affluent, fashion-conscious homes, a tradition evolved for bridegrooms to present their new wives with a set of English wallpapers.

On one level, the eighteenth century was a golden age for wallpaper. Carefully made by skilled craftsmen, it was loved by the rich and could be found decorating the smartest of homes. However, as the nineteenth century dawned, it became clear that if the industry was really to succeed it had to find a way of printing continuous rolls of paper quickly enough to make wallpaper affordable for all. Mechanisation beckoned.

The first commercially successful wallpaper-printing machine was patented in Britain in 1839 by calico printing firm Potters and Ross. The paper was drawn over the surface of a large central drum and then the pattern was applied using a number of engraved metal cylinders, which were fed with coloured pigment stored in a trough beneath them. The first cylinders were made of copper and had designs cut into the metal but they couldn't produce solid blocks of colour so, in the 1840s, the company switched to wooden rollers which had the pattern raised on the surface. When solid blocks of colour were required the rollers were simply packed with felt.

Aesthetically, the results were poor compared with hand-blocked papers but what the new machine-printed papers lacked in quality was more than made up for in quantity. In 1834, for example, the British wallpaper industry produced 1,222,753 rolls of paper; by 1851, ten years after the first machine-printed papers went on sale, output had risen to 5,500,000 rolls and by 1874 it had reached 32 million. The most significant impact of this increase in production was on cost. By the 1850s you could pick up a roll of wallpaper for sixpence. Wallpaper as a democratic decorating device was born.

Machine printing didn't only increase production, it also had a profound effect on the designs that could be used. Hand blocking produced rich colours but machine printing allowed for detail on a scale not previously achievable. In France, technological advances sparked a fashion for papers featuring trompe l'oeil swags of opulent fabric, while in Britain, manufacturers used mechanisation to produce papers strewn with hyper-real flowers. The average Victorian homeowner loved them, covering living room walls with cabbage roses so realistic they appeared three-dimensional.

Not everyone welcomed wallpaper's cheap, super-real, new world. For design reformers such as A.W.N. Pugin and his successor Owen

Jones lowering prices meant lowering standards, while naturalistic motifs were the great lies of the design world. Walls, they argued, are flat and should therefore be covered with patterns that emphasised rather than disguised their two dimensionality. These were powerful voices and the fashion cognoscenti took note. Wallpaper was still acceptable, so long as it bore Pugin's much-loved Gothic architectural motifs or the Arts and Crafts Movement's stylised florals, but it was no longer chic.

Its survival through the twentieth century can be attributed almost entirely to the mass market. There were brief flurries of interest from the design world. In the 1930s well-known architects and designers began to collaborate with manufacturers to produce abstracted, geometric designs (in Germany, for example, Rasch produced a collection of papers in conjunction with Modernist design school, The Bauhaus), and the 1950s saw a surge of architectural interest resulting in American company Schumacher working with Frank Lloyd Wright and British company Sanderson launching Palladio, an abstract range specifically aimed at architects. But these were moments only. For most of the century the industry concentrated on turning out cheap paper that was easy to clean (wipeable vinyl papers first appeared in 1947), easy to put up (pre-pasted papers hit the DIY world in the 1950s) and cheap to buy.

Fortunately, by the late 1990s, when even the mass market had begun to eschew papered walls in favour of minimal paint, there were designers appearing who seemed ready to re-invent wallpaper for the new millennium. Well-versed in wallpaper's history (but crucially not in awe of it), people such as Brit-based designers Sharon Elphick and Deborah Bowness began to use new digital technology to produce the kind of statement-making feature wallpaper not seen since the French panoramics of the late nineteenth century.

Two decades on, wallpaper is enjoying a real renaissance. There are papers referencing – and sometimes precisely replicating – every historical style from flock to toile du Jouy and they're available at prices pitched to every budget. There are even papers which pretend to be something else – a brick wall, a wooded glade, a filing cabinet – but now such imitations are seen as amusing and ironic rather than symbols of moral decline. Five centuries after it first appeared, wallpaper has become both a respected art form and an accepted way of updating a room on the cheap.

Chapter 1

Architectural Illusions

Wallpaper has always created illusions. After all, it owes its very existence to the middle classes' desire for a cheaper alternative to the tapestries, panelling and architectural flourishes favoured by the aristocracy.

The first paper imitating plasterwork appeared in England in the late seventeenth century, but it wasn't until the middle of the next century that architecturally inspired papers really found their place – due in large part to the fact that, while house builders favoured rooms with plain walls, house buyers still preferred panels, dados and mouldings. French manufacturer Durolin was one of the leading makers of the time, selling sheets of paper columns, cornices and architraves, designed to be cut out and pasted to the wall in an early version of today's easy-peel wall stickers.

Architectural papers of this period fell into two styles: Gothic, and classical pillar and arch. Gothic papers, popular in Britain, France and Germany, started out as simple and realistic imitations of stonework effects, but by the 1820s the style had moved on to include rather fanciful vignettes of ruined buildings and statuary, which consumers hung about their homes with scant regard for scale and proportion.

Pillar and arch papers, with their elaborate arcades and imposing sculptures, were a largely British creation. As pieces of art, these papers were both interesting and impressive; as wallcoverings however, they were hard to live with, since they created distorted perspectives. Fortunately for the manufacturers, consumers seemed to enjoy the effect – especially in America where the style attracted something of a cult following.

Until the middle of the nineteenth century that is, when such blatantly imitative wallpaper came under fire from the Design Reform Movement. Vehemently critical of what Reformers regarded as the genre's dishonesty, they advocated flat designs that emphasised, rather than disguised, the two-dimensional nature of walls.

The kind of flat, graphic papers championed by the Design Reform Movement quickly found a market that has remained constant to this day. In the 1930s, for example, they were produced by European Modernists (including the arch enemy of decoration, Le Corbusier), while the 1950s saw a fashion for papers featuring curved calligraphic lines combined with small abstract and geometric motifs.

Today, graphic wallpapers are amongst the most exciting and best-selling styles on the market, appealing to people tired of minimalism but reluctant to relinquish the clean simplicity of plain walls. Contemporary wallpaper designer Natasha Marshall, who specialises in graphic prints, puts the continuing appeal of the style down to its timelessness and flexibility. 'Graphic wallpapers complement the architecture of a building, enhancing a space rather than taking over,' she says. 'And they are completely timeless.'

EMBOSSED PAPERS

Embossed wallpaper – the textured wallcoverings that, in the twentieth century, became the favourite cover-up for anyone cursed with an uneven wall – first appeared in the 1840s. By 1860 French manufacturer Paul Balin was using the new technique (in which paper was pressure-stamped with either blocks, plates or rollers) to produce startlingly realistic imitations of silk and embroidered textiles, but it was three inventions in the subsequent decades that finally propelled embossed paper from niche product to mass market must-have.

Lincrusta Walton was the first. Created in 1877 by Frederick Walton, the man behind linoleum, it was made primarily from relief printed, solidified linseed oil backed initially with heavy canvas then, a few years later, with paper. This was a crucial development: as a lightweight product, Lincrusta could be used not only in public buildings (where its waterproof qualities made it hygienic enough for hospitals and tough enough for railway carriages) but in private homes as well. Far cheaper than real relief plasterwork, Lincrusta was used to bring some architectural splendour to flat walls and ceilings in the halls and dining rooms of the upper middle class.

Anaglypta, invented in 1886 by T.J. Palmer, gave the mass market its chance to experiment with embossed papers. Rather than embossing the finished paper, as was the case with Lincrusta, Anaglypta was made by embossing paper pulp on a paper-making machine. Not only was this a simpler (and therefore cheaper) method of production, but the final product was also made with a hollow relief, making it incredibly light and easy to use. Anaglypta was an instant success. By the end of the century, Potters (which had taken over the company in 1894) was routinely receiving more than 100 orders a day.

The style's lasting success was guaranteed in 1911 when British wallpaper manufacturing giant Sanderson patented the first wallpaper embossing machine. By roller embossing paper, the company was able to make textured wallcoverings for a fraction of the price of both Lincrusta and Anaglypta. And what's more, thanks to the arrival of easy-clean homes, due to the introduction of electric vacuum cleaners and electric (rather than coal) heating, it was able to offer them in a range of light, refreshing colours. The market responded: in 1920s suburbia, pastel-toned embossed paper was the hottest look around.

How and Where to Use

Forget porridge-toned hessian and pattern-clashing flocks; today's textured papers are sophisticated (think real leather), innovative (think crystal beads on a backing so pliable it wraps around corners) and superbly glamorous (think giant flocked prints in hot house colours). But they're not all that easy to use because, along with the usual issues of where to hang dramatic papers, there's the added complication of how to make wood grain, grass cloth or funkily flocked paper stick to the wall. As professional paper hanger Yair Meshoulam explains, textured papers call for strong adhesive, a felt roller (standard brushes damage the surface) and a cautious hand, as stray spots of glue can't be wiped off. It's worth the effort though: textured papers are the most flexible wallcoverings around.

METALLICS
Guaranteed to inject a dose of urban bling into any room it graces, metallic wallpaper represents textured paper at its most contemporary. That space-enhancing, glossy surface makes it the perfect foil for dense pattern so you can wrap it right around a room without closing down the space; you can afford to have some fun with the furnishings. Invest in some high-gloss furniture to reflect those mirror-like walls, then add a shaggy rug for some softening textural contrast.

FLOCK

Flock was once a wallcovering reserved only for the wealthy, but, thanks to the recent explosion in inventive technology, it is now accessible to all and the great thing is that the affordable machine-made versions still have all the luxurious glamour of their handmade predecessors. (They are, however, prone to crushing, so avoid flocking walls in heavy traffic areas such as hallways.)

There's no such thing as understated flock. Patterns tend towards over-sized damasks and extravagant baroque scrollwork, while colours tend to be rich and vibrant. (Lime green and hot pink are contemporary favourites.) And now, according to Shauna Dennison, Wallpapers Design Manager at British wallpaper company Osborne & Little, we're also beginning to see quite architectural and geometric designs appearing, as companies become more daring and inventive with imagery.

The easiest way to use such over-the-top wallcoverings is to confine them to a single feature area. Choose a large, flat wall unencumbered by architectural features such as windows and doorways (they're hard to paper round) and treat the remaining walls as a backdrop that subtly echoes the texture and tones of the dominant wall.

However, as the owner of the bedroom above proves, flock can also look fabulous wrapped right around a room. The secret of success is to thoroughly embrace the extravagance of the style (half-hearted opulence is not a good look) so, when it comes to furnishings, go for chandeliers, mirrors and as many sumptuous cushions as you can afford. The only limitation should be the colour scheme: sticking to a single shade will ensure your room stays just the right side of kitsch.

COLE & SON

Founded in Britain in 1873, Cole & Son – or John Perry Ltd as the company was originally called – became famous for several innovative new wallpaper techniques, but it was owner John Perry's decision to bring back flocked papers in the 1870s which has gone down as one of the company's most lasting achievements.

Originally invented in Holland in 1680 as a way of copying the Belgian tapestries so popular amongst the aristocracy, flock became enormously popular both in Britain and continental Europe. Opulent and reminiscent of cut and stamped velvet, it was the perfect wallcovering for the rising merchant classes who wanted the look, but couldn't quite afford the expense, of real fabric.

Cole & Son's flock wallpaper was made entirely by hand. It was a simple, if time-consuming and hazardous, procedure (it wasn't uncommon for people to die as a result of inhaling the wool fibres), involving block-printing with slow-drying adhesive onto plain paper and then sieving powdered wool over the glue design as it passed through a wooden trough. The flocked paper was then hung out to dry, brushed down and rolled into 10 metre lengths.

Having enjoyed a reputation as a top end wallcovering for over 200 years, flock's status went into free fall in the late 1940s thanks to its ubiquitous use in Britain's curry houses. As Anthony Evans, Managing Director of Cole & Son says, 'Flock was a sensationally marvellous product up until the end of World War II, then it was taken up by the Indian and Chinese restaurants and its reputation fell into a black hole.'

Cole & Son continued to make flock wallpaper during the wilderness years, supplying the rather controversial paper for former British Lord Chancellor Lord Irvine's rooms in Westminster Palace, London and in 2000 it took the decision to celebrate the fact that it was the only company in the world still making flock in the traditional way and target a whole new market: a market made up of people too young to remember flocked curry houses and design conscious enough to recognise that handmade wallpaper doesn't come cheap. It was the right move: today, using a sieve dating back to 1925, Cole & Son is producing cutting edge flock paper that proves traditional methods are no bar to contemporary design.

OTHER TEXTURAL OPTIONS

Almost anything can be turned into a wallcovering - leather, wood, sea grass and even beads and sequins are readily available and all will bring visual interest as well as a feeling of warmth and sensual comfort to a space.

However, the best thing about these papers is that they allow you to do the wallpaper thing without having to embrace full-on pattern. (The worst is that some of them are a real challenge to clean so, if you don't like dusting, avoid anything too multi-layered.) As British wallpaper designer and textural expert Tracy Kendall says, 'Purely textural papers aren't overcrowded with design so they add details and balance to a room without taking over.' And that makes them fantastically easy to live with. Use on all four walls as a subtle backdrop to paintings, mirrors and ornaments (don't be afraid of hanging pictures on leather walls: leather specialists Bill Amberg recommend filling old holes with wax then buffing the surface in a matching colour) or turn the paper into the main story by using it on a single feature wall. And if you like the idea of a textural feature but can't face pasting up, simply do as the owner of the sitting room shown far left has done and pin one drop, picture-style to the top of the wall.

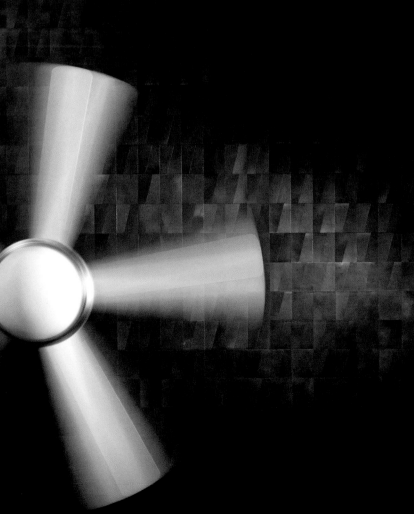

MAYA ROMANOFF

Founded in Chicago in 1969, the Maya Romanoff Corporation set out to transform modern design by combining ancient artistic techniques with the latest production technology. And it has. From the outset, the company has pushed technological boundaries to produce truly unique wallcoverings such as 'Precious Metals', made by applying metal leaf to paper with chopsticks, and 'Beadazzled Flexible Glass Bead Wallcovering™': a paper so ground-breaking that it is on permanent display in the Cooper Hewitt National Design Museum in New York.

Exactly how 'Beadazzled' is made is a closely guarded secret. All Maya Romanoff will reveal is that the glass beads are mounted on light-reflective foil backings so that they create a shimmering luminosity even in the most dimly lit of interiors. However, the result of what Romanoff describes as 'manufacturing breakthroughs' is a glass bead wallcovering flexible enough to be wrapped around corners , light enough to be cut with standard wallpapering tools and which can be removed without destroying the wall.

'Beadazzled' was created in 2002 and it was such a success that the Maya Romanoff Corporation has been experimenting with beading and patterning techniques ever since. 'Geode', for example, is composed of masses of multi-sized beads while 'Bauble' features the biggest beads – a show stopping 4mm in diameter – ever used on a wallcovering to date.

Of course, these are not papers for the average family home but their popularity with the world's most forward-thinking interior designers has meant that its products are found all over the world from Nobu in Hong Kong, Melbourne and Los Angeles to the palace of the Crown Prince of Dubai.

ARCHITECTURAL TROMPE L'OEIL

Wallpaper has always been imitative and these days digital printing has enabled designers to create papers so realistic you have to actually feel them before you can be sure of what you are seeing.

Many of these papers are about providing some subtle texture and enabling the user to create effects that would be too costly or impractical to achieve otherwise - after all, paper look-alike marble or stonework is very much easier to buy, apply and live with than the real thing.

Others are designed to be the dominant decorative force in a room. Deborah Bowness's 'Illusions of Grandeur' wallpaper (above) depicts a ready decorated wall, complete with fake decorative dado and skirting board. 'I take a photographic montage, enlarge it to life size then reproduce it in black and white onto a wallpaper,' explains Bowness. 'I then colour the paper by hand using silk screen printing techniques. The idea is not to reproduce exactly but to represent familiar interior imagery, patterns and architecture to create an illusion of grandeur that can be used in any space.'

ARCHITECTURAL TROMPE L'OEIL

Papers imitating wood and brickwork provide warmth, texture and a distinctly architectural take on pattern. The key to using these papers successfully is to think of them not as wallpaper at all but as the material they represent, so if you wouldn't dream of cladding your entire bathroom in grainy pine don't cover it in a paper version of grainy pine either. As the images here illustrate, wood and exposed bricks are tailor-made for feature walls. (They are also particularly effective in narrow rooms where they have the effect of widening the space.) Let your chosen paper become the dominant decorative force in the room and, when it comes to furnishing, think textural contrast: rough bricks with smooth leather, soft wood with hard metal, shiny veneer with shaggy textiles. And as for the remaining walls, go for paint in a toning shade or take the texture thing to the limit and combine with sea grass or hessian in a similar colour.

A.W.N. PUGIN (1812–1852)

Augustus Welby Northmore Pugin had a dream: a passionate
advocate of medieval art and architecture, he wanted to take
Gothic design to the masses. The masses had already discovered
Gothic of course – wallpapers imitating Gothic architecture were
the height of fashion in the 1840s – but Pugin was a purist. To
him, the use of trompe l'oeil effects to turn flat walls into faux
Gothic buildings was not only in poor taste but was morally
reprehensible too. In his view, Gothic designs must be historically
accurate and, more importantly, be used to enhance rather than
disguise a wall's inherent flatness.

'A wall may be enriched or decorated at pleasure,' he
explained, 'but it must always be treated in a consistent manner.'
His views were radical at the time – the mid 1800s was an eclectic
period, and as far as historic inspiration was concerned, tastes
were more for pastiche than accuracy – and they didn't help him
achieve his dream. So, while Pugin was a success as a designer (in
1847 he was commissioned to create over 100 wallpapers for the
Palace of Westminster and his distinctive prints with their heavily
stylised fruit and foliage designs and heraldic emblems were
enormously popular amongst the aristocracy), his dream of taking
Gothic design to the masses was never realised. This was partly
due to the cost (his papers were all hand printed), but his patterns
were also considered too ecclesiastical for average tastes and when
the craze for all things Gothic passed in the 1850s, Pugin's papers
had made little impact on public taste.

His design legacy however has had lasting influence. By the
end of the nineteenth century Pugin's assertion that wallpaper
should be flat and not excessively naturalistic had been accepted
as the standard principal of wallpaper design and in the wider
design world his theories formed the basis of the Design Reform
Movement, which in turn influenced the Modernists of the
twentieth century.

'What Pugin did,' explains Joanna Banham, Head of Adult
Learning at the Victoria and Albert Museum and author of an
essay on Pugin's wallpaper, 'was to stand up and rail against the
rampant eclecticism of a period in which there was no theory of
design, just rather a lot of bad taste. He argued for more discipline
and rationalism in design.' Attributes that remain the foundation
of good design today.

GRAPHIC PRINTS

Graphic wallpaper is fantastically flexible. The clean lines and simple, repeating forms which characterise the genre mean that, depending on how you use them, graphic papers can be either quiet backdrops or statement-making central features. Rather surprisingly, more is less with the majority of these papers: as the sternly monochrome paper in the bedroom above shows, used in abundance a repeating pattern can lose its intensity and take on a rhythm that's positively soothing to live with. Confined to a single wall, on the other hand, graphic papers become central features, defining specific zones within a multi-functional room (see the home-office space opposite) or simply injecting a dose of pattern into an otherwise plain space.

MIXING PRINTS

Contemporary, bold and soothing when used on a large scale, symmetrical repeating prints are made for mixing. Try using a simple geometric motif as a backdrop to paintings or collections of ornaments (the striped paper in the image above gives the collection of hanging plates a modern edge and provides a clean contrast to the floral prints) or do as the owner of the house pictured above left has done and set print against print to make pattern the main decorative theme of the space.

RASCH

The 1950s was a decade of innovation for German wallpaper company Rasch. Having started life in the late 1800s as a manufacturer of oil cloths, Emil Rasch – Rouleauxfabric, as the company was then known, soon diversified into wallpapers and by the beginning of the twentieth century was a leading player in the mass market.

Rasch's wallpapers may have been inexpensive but the company was determined to prove low prices were no bar to artistic merit.

'It is not just a question of launching goods on to the domestic market at relatively cheap prices,' Rasch said, 'but also of offering buyers something of artistic value.'

What Emil Rasch offered was the Artist's Collection. Launched in 1950, the idea was to ask leading contemporary artists, designers and architects to translate their personal vision into a domestic decorating project. The collections continued until 1960 by which time over 50 top names had collaborated with Rasch, including Josef Hoffmann, Tea Ernst, Margret Hildebrand, Lucienne Day and Salvador Dalì. The results were a mix of figurative prints and abstract, graphic patterns all quite different from the easy florals that had dominated the mainstream wallpaper industry for so many years. Lucienne Day's 'Prisma' print, for example, was an austere tangle of criss-crossing lines while Margret Hildebrand's best-selling 'Studie' featured abstracted five-fingered leaves.

The high point for the Artist's Collection came in 1956 when Rasch staged an exhibition entitled Creative Art – Industrial Design at the City Museum of Osnabruck. Featuring papers by 28 of the artists involved in the project, the show sought to display wallpaper as art rather than as mere background decoration. The exhibition was a huge success, so much so that Rasch was asked to take it to New York where it gave fresh impetus to the declining American wallpaper industry.

Not everyone welcomed wallpaper's new artistic status. The press, for example, were scathing in their reporting of the exhibition. 'It's really quite hilarious,' wrote the *Industriekurier* on August 11th, 1956. 'Something that would be disparagingly dismissed as modern art in the form of a framed oil painting is a great success when depicted on rolls of paper.'

But Rasch was not to be put off. He believed in what he was doing and also considered that, as a manufacturer of wallpaper, it was his job to give the public what they wanted rather than what he (or the art press) considered they should want. And sales of the Artist's Collection proved that post war German homeowners wanted abstracted graphic prints.

DAVID OLIVER

In 1989 British designer David Oliver wallpapered his house. But instead of conventional wallpaper, Oliver used newspaper – a pleasingly coloured mix of the *Financial Times*, *Sydney Morning Herald* and *Yellow Pages* – into which he cut various floral shapes so that the wall beneath the paper, rather than the paper itself, became the repeating pattern.

It was the start of a fascination with decorating walls and the graphic possibilities of newspaper. Three years later, he made a series of drawings based on the shapes of the text, advertisements and photographs of the French newspaper *Liberation* for an art gallery in Madrid. 'The drawings unveiled the skeleton or underlying shapes present in the layout of a newspaper,' Oliver explains. 'The shapes were strangely familiar and the beauty of the project lay in the discovery of a pattern that is not always seen because of the way in which we read.'

In 1998 this pattern was launched as a wallpaper. 'Liberation', as it was called in memory of the paper which inspired it, featured repeating geometric blocks in subtle colours. At a time when minimalism was the height of chic and wallpaper was synonymous with outmoded busyness, 'Liberation's clean rhythmic print represented a new aesthetic and proved that pattern could have a place in pared-down contemporary homes. Low-key it may be, but 'Liberation' became an instant design classic and played a key part in wallpaper's return to fashionability.

Even the most extravagant eye-popping patterns can be made to look pared down and (relatively) simple: it's just a question of how they are used and what they're mixed with. In this dining room, for example, the pattern has been stretched right across a long back wall to maximise its rhythmic symmetry and make it easier on the eye. A row of chandeliers and a set of identical dining chairs echo the repetitive, geometric theme and give the room a contemporary sense of low-key opulence.

What goes up must come down.

Watch Super Fresco go up on TV to the music of the famous song "What goes up must come down."
It will set your customers' feet tapping and their hands itching to get this super high relief wallcovering. "That flat back," as the commercial says "firmly put in its place, press it down, it bounces back."

Sales go up, stocks come down.

Sales quadrupled when Super Fresco went up on TV in Granada, Tyne Tees and Ulster in the Spring. Now a bigger TV burst goes into London, Central, Scotland – and Granada and Tyne Tees again – from September 26th to October 12th, just before the re-decorating season for millions.
Ask now for free Point of Sale material.
Over 20 ways of great relief patterns. And it's British.

super Fresco

It's by Graham and Brown.

GRAHAM AND BROWN LTD, P.O. BOX 39, INDIA MILL, HARWOOD STREET, BLACKBURN, LANCASHIRE BB1 3DB.

GRAHAM & BROWN

British wallpaper company Graham & Brown was founded on a mixture of vision and serendipity: 1946 was a lean year for wallpaper companies (paper was in short supply after the war), so when two aspiring entrepreneurs, Harold Graham and Henry Brown, came across a stack of decommissioned metallic papers which had been used by the army to foil enemy radar, they bought the lot and a business was born.

Their factory at Harwood Street, Blackburn was cramped and basic, containing little more than an embossing machine and an eight-colour surface printer, but the public were so hungry for pretty papers to brighten up their post-war homes – and pretty papers were so hard to find – that Graham & Brown soon became a major player in the wallpaper world.

By the 1970s, the company was producing millions of rolls of affordably priced wallpaper every year and it had established itself as one of Britain's largest independent wallpaper manufacturers, as well as a growing force in Europe. But the Seventies was a tough decade for wallpaper: as more and more homeowners turned to DIY, paint took over from paper as the wall covering of choice. Graham & Brown's solution was to innovate: in 1984 the company (under the joint direction of Roger Graham and David Brown, sons of the original founders) launched Superfresco, a textured vinyl collection of papers that were easy to hang, easy to strip and could be washed and painted too.

This was the first wallpaper range the company chose to advertise. The TV ad with its catchy slogan 'what goes up, must come down' became something of an icon and ensured the paper became an instant hit. A year later, Superfresco had quadrupled the company's market share and tripled its turnover.

With nine rolls now being sold every minute and international sales topping £10 million a year, Superfresco is still the company's most successful line – and, so it claims, the world's most favourite wallpaper. New variations have been launched, including Superfresco Easy which, because you paste the wall rather than the paper, is quicker and cleaner to hang than ever before. And for a new generation of DIYers, eager to cover up imperfect walls with a bit of retro chic, that's is what it's all about.

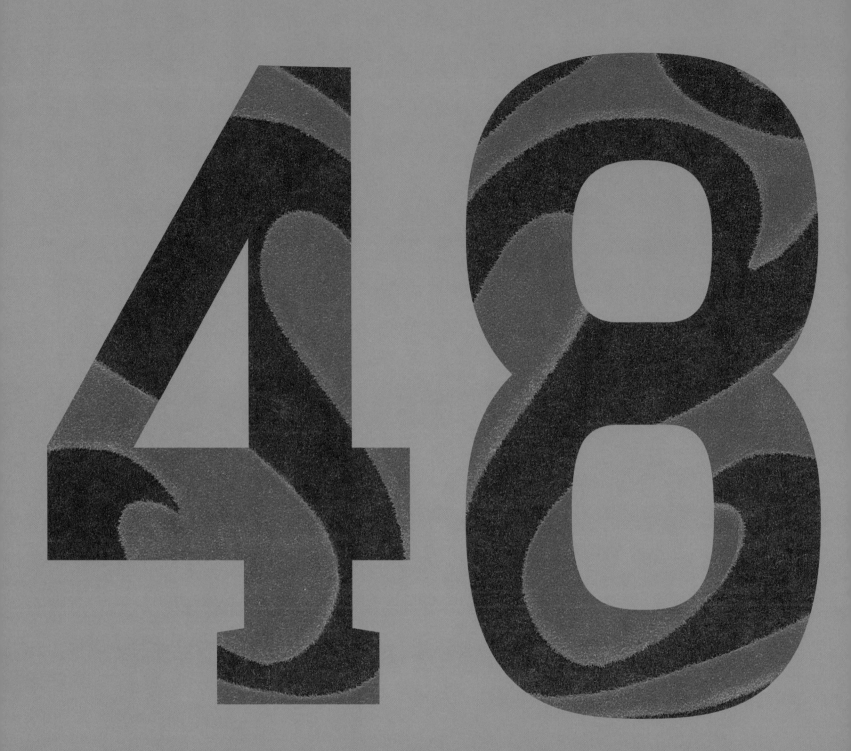

Beautiful contemporary architectural wallpapers to brighten your life.

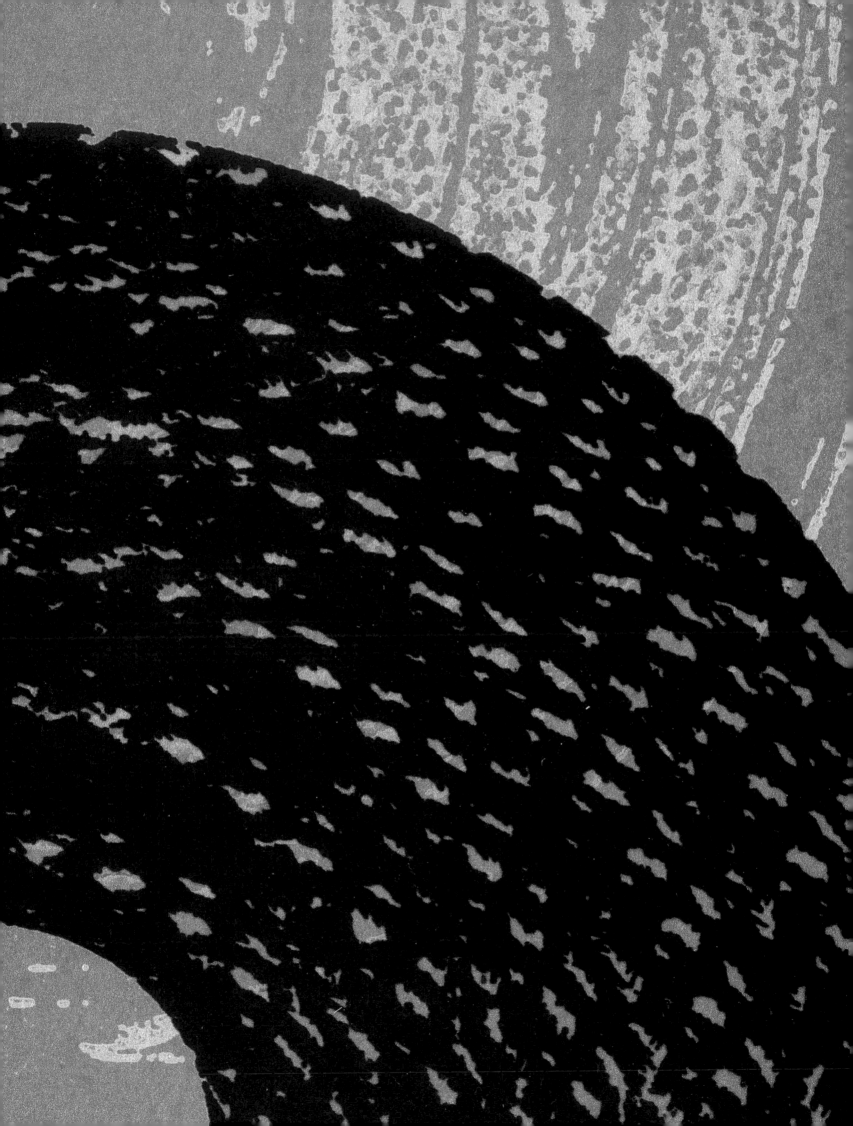

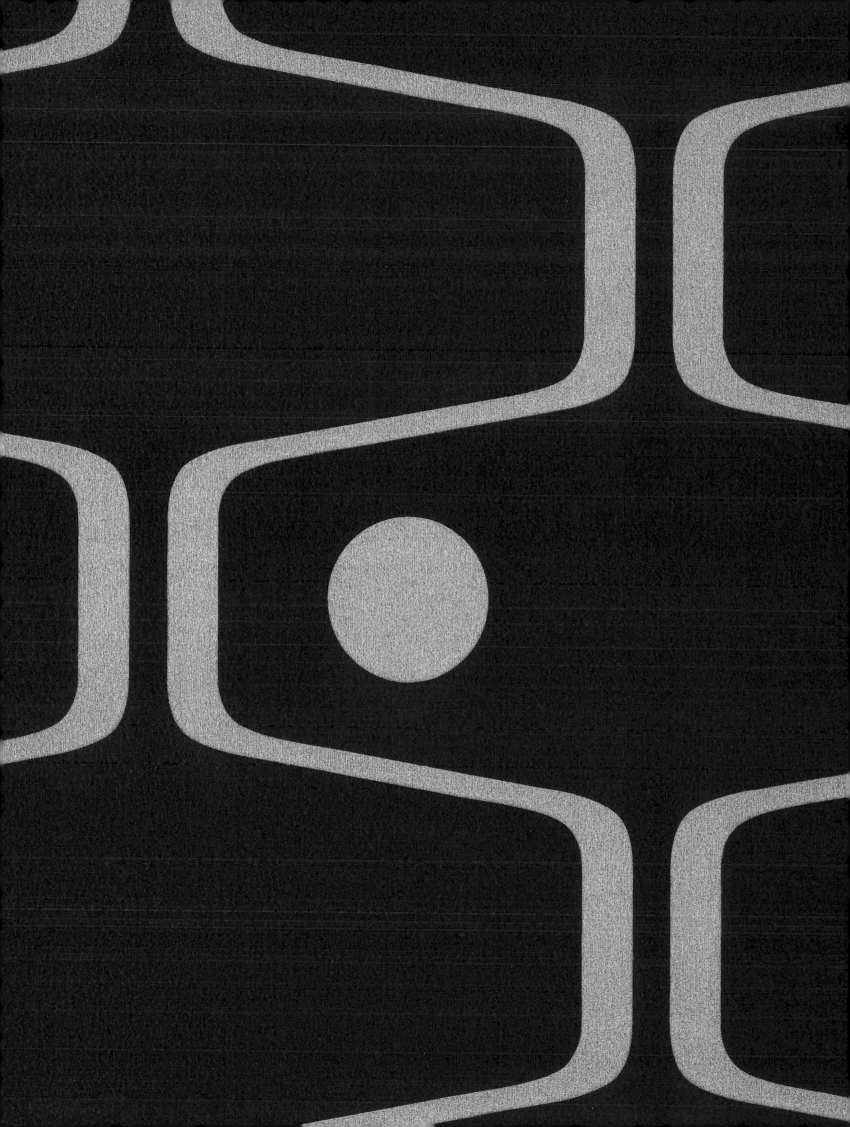

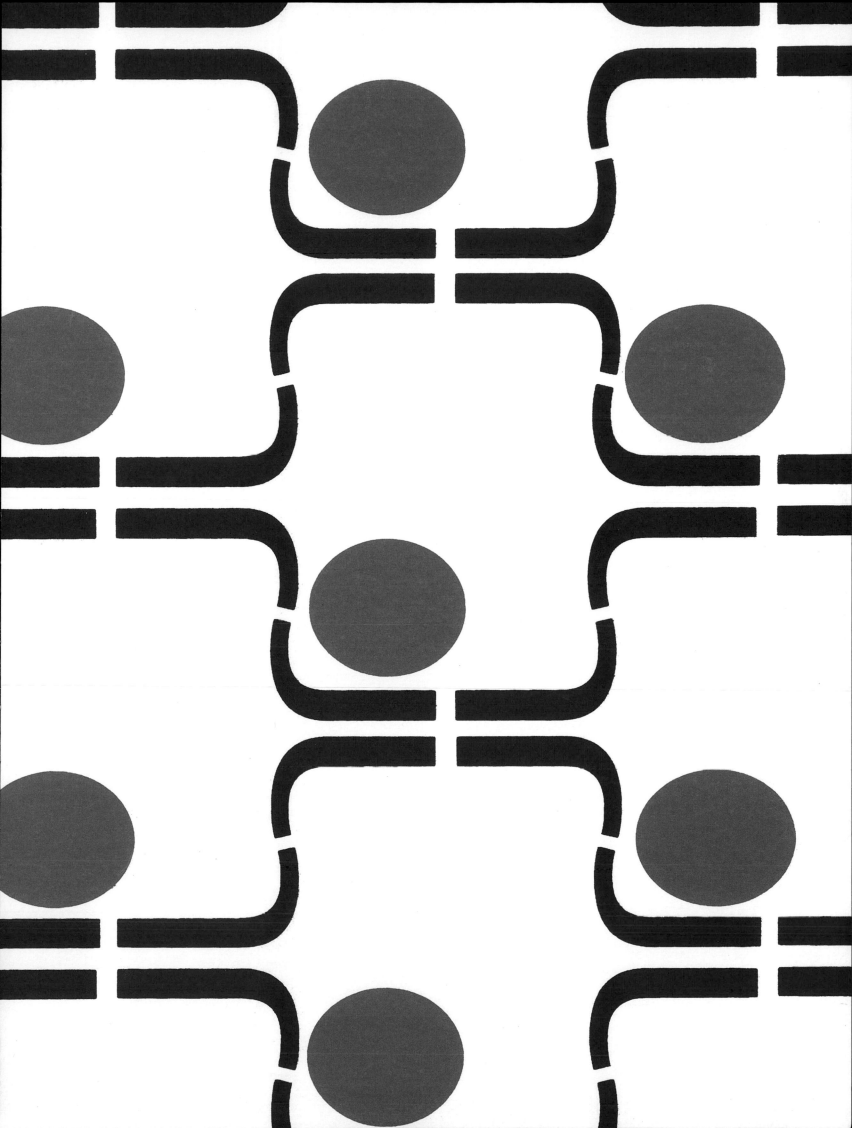

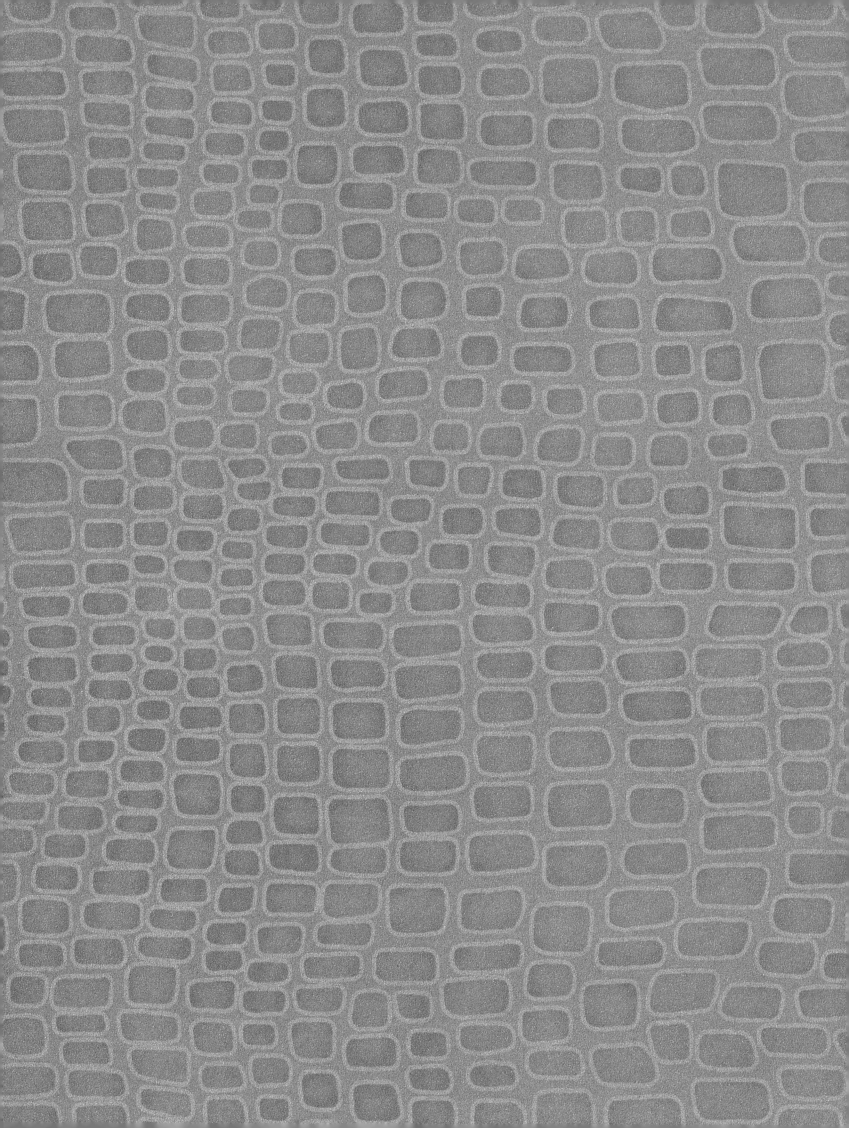

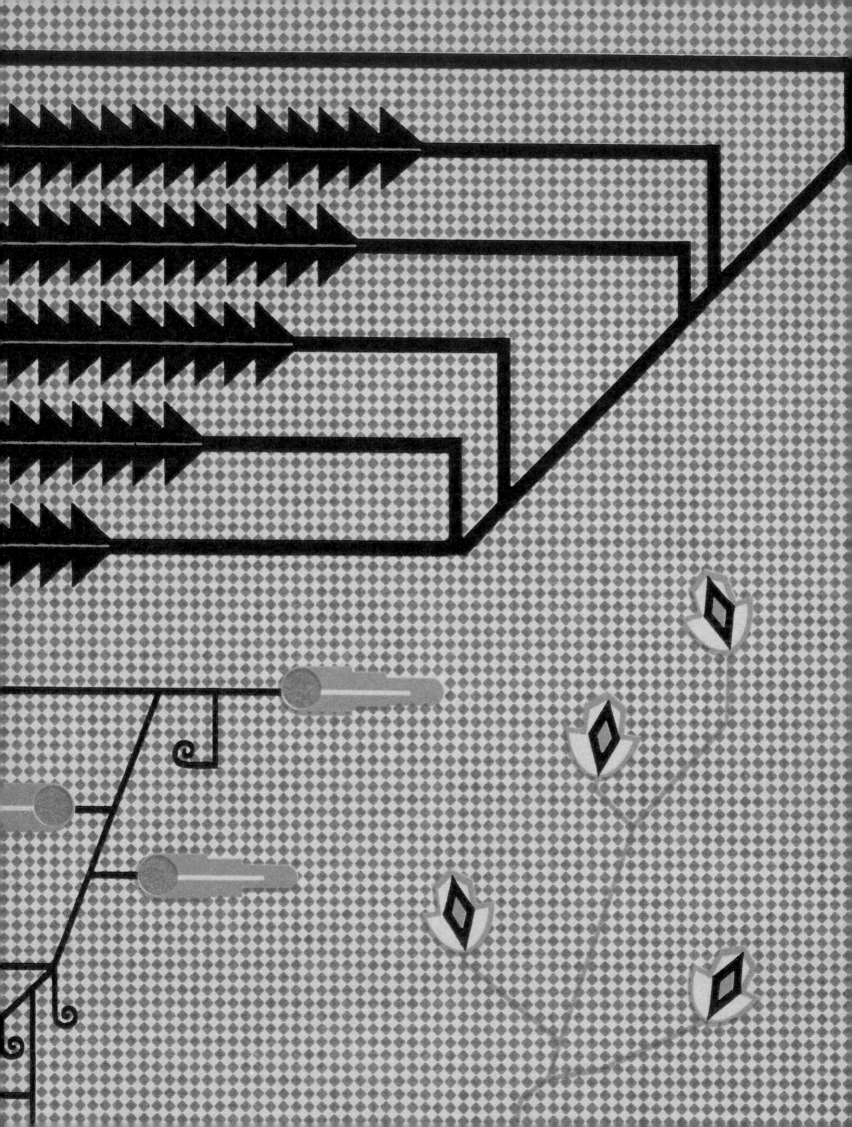

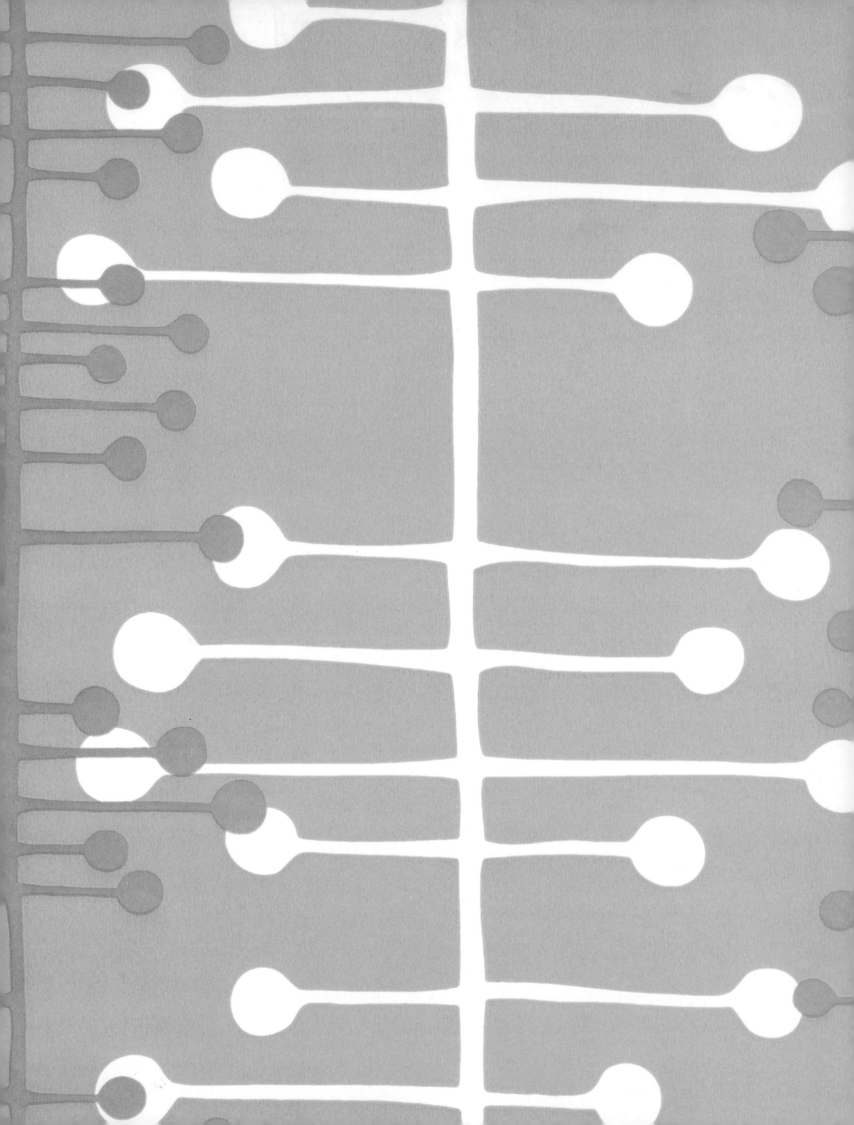

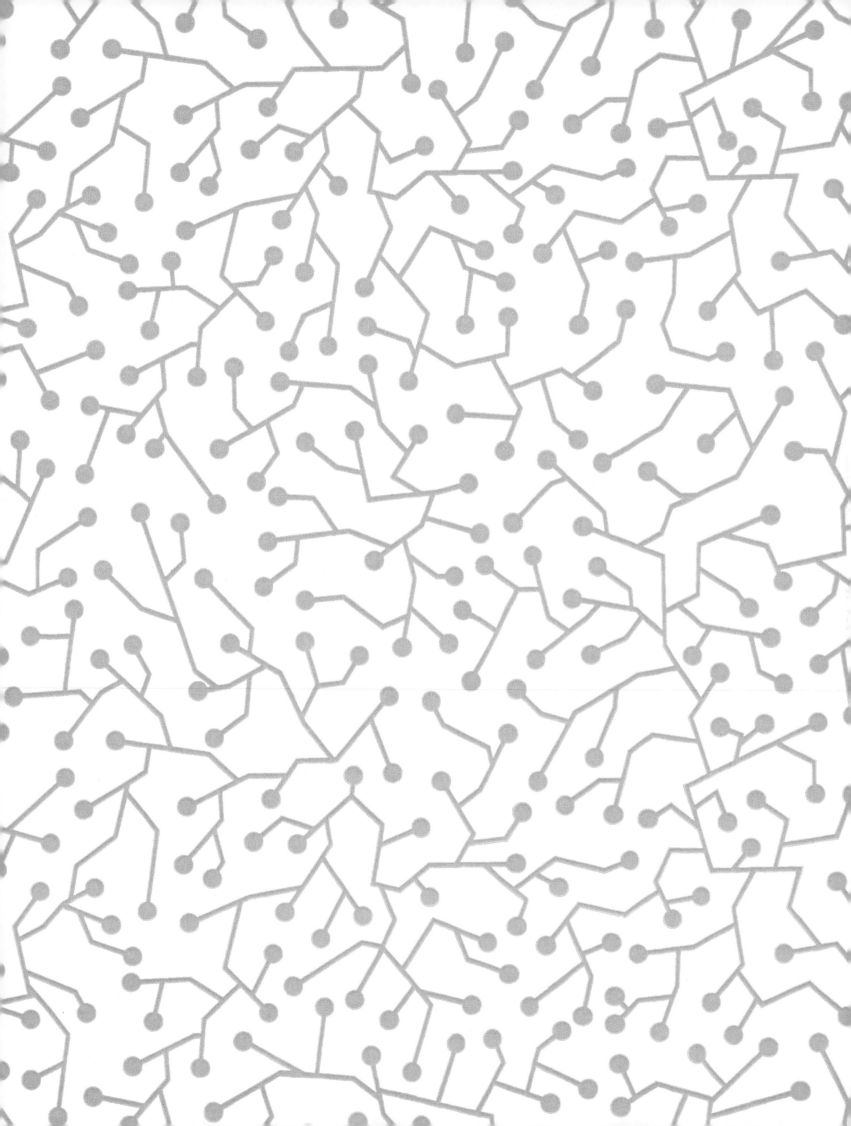

Fabulous Florals

Flowers are probably the most universally popular of all decorative motifs. Delicate or imposing, subtly coloured or hot house bright, flowers – and the foliage surrounding them – have been inspiring artists and designers for centuries. As Shauna Dennison, Wallpapers Design Manager at British design house Osborne & Little says, 'Flowers are the most benign things you can think of in terms of decoration, but they are also great vehicles for pattern and print and come in a variety of sizes so you can have both large- and small-scale repeats.' Which, in design terms, makes them the perfect motif.

Small, sprig-strewn designs inspired by printed cottons and muslins were the first floral motifs to be translated onto wallpaper. Radical they were not and cutting-edge designers throughout history have largely spurned these pretty, simple papers, but they have been consistently popular with mid-market manufacturers and consumers since the early eighteenth century. Technically, small floral repeats were the most straightforward type of pattern to print, both with wooden blocks and the early wallpaper printing machines, while, aesthetically, consumers have always been drawn to their unchallenging familiarity and go-with-anything ease.

However, sprigged wallpapers have had their high-fashion moments. Regency Britain adopted them with a passion, combining them with vertical stripes towards the end of the period for a cooler, more graphic take on the look, and in the mid-nineteenth century, style conscious bedrooms throughout Europe were all sporting small-scale floral papers on their walls.

The 1970s were a boom time too: in Britain, Laura Ashley launched its first collection of country cottage-style papers in 1973 and in 1978, Coloroll launched 'Dolly Mixtures', a miniaturised floral design by Linda Beard that swiftly became the country's best-selling wallpaper design.

The Noughties have not been kind to the small floral repeats: modern floral wallpaper is all about drama on a grand scale. And not for the first time – big, bold floral prints have a well-established history which dates back to eighteenth-century France.

Flowers emerged as the country's most favourite wallpaper motif in around 1780. Designs ranged from the naturalistic to the highly stylised and the papers they adorned came both as decorative borders, designed to frame panels of plain paper, and as full rolls, intended to be used on all four walls of a room. Roses were the most popular motif (roses have always been our favourite variety of flower due to their appealing round shape) and they were always depicted in full bloom, as perfectionism personified. These were top quality papers, hand block printed with meticulous attention to detail. Popular amongst the emerging bourgeoisie in France, the style swept across middle-class

Europe, only to be challenged in Britain in the 1860s by the graphically orientated Design Reformers such as Owen Jones and the simple-is-best Arts and Crafts designer William Morris.

The twentieth century was harder on florals, both large and small. The Modern Movement derided ornamentation in any form and the 1950s and 1960s were dominated by abstract, graphic prints rather than flowers. However, as the twenty first century dawned, big, statement-making floral designs were making a comeback and it's a style that looks set to stay. 'Flowers have traditionally been perceived as feminine,' explains Shauna Dennison, 'but they are now starting to take on a much more masculine look. The designs are becoming less colourful and blowsy and roses are giving way to more architectural motifs such as leaves, fronds and allium heads.' This spiky, monochrome take on flowery wallpaper may be a new departure but its roots lie firmly in our centuries old love of all things floral.

CHINTZ

Chintz has become synonymous with a certain type of Englishness: those blowsy cabbage roses scattered abundantly over pastel-coloured grounds are the very essence of Cotswold cottage chic. But chintz is, in fact, an Indian creation.

Originally a calico fabric painted with floral or, less commonly, pictorial patterns in brilliant, vibrant shades, chintz (or chint as it was known in India) was discovered by European adventurers in the seventeenth century and imported into the continent by the East India Company. It was an instant success: to a people used to a decorative diet of dark, heavy fabrics these fresh and lively cottons represented an altogether lighter way to live.

The first European chintz fabrics were produced in Marseilles then, shortly afterwards, in London. The fledgling British industry received a huge boost when, in 1700, the wool and silk manufacturers imposed a law banning the use of Indian silks and calicos for domestic use on pain of a £200 fine. The effect of the ban was two-fold: it helped to shore up the British textile industry as intended but, by making chintz less readily available, it also presented the wallpaper manufacturers with an exciting opportunity. If the public's new found taste for vibrant colour couldn't be satisfied with fabric then they would satisfy it with paper. Chintz-style wallpaper was born.

How and Where to Use

It's been a long time since any trend-aware homeowner has contemplated decorating with anything more than a burst of floral pattern. After all, we chucked out our chintz and stripped off the matching borders as the 1980s drew to a close and have been inhabiting a world of tasteful plainness ever since. But exuberant, wall-to-wall pattern is making a comeback and this time around anything goes, from clashing prints to strict co-ordination. Full-on floral is a bold look (get it wrong and you end up with visual chaos) but done well, it's vibrant, exciting and unmistakably twenty-first century. So what's the secret of success?

PATTERN EXPLOSION
The first step is to decide how many patterns you're going to use. The owners of the rooms shown on these pages have gone for a single print which they have used in abundance, not only on all the walls but across the doors and, in the bedroom on the right, over the ceiling as well. The effect of all this extravagant pattern is to turn these two small and otherwise featureless rooms into rich, jewel box-like spaces that delight and surprise. A spare approach to furniture in both rooms ensures that the pattern takes centre stage and avoids visual overload. The glossy reflective surfaces and white ceiling in the dining room, above, keep the mood light and modern.

Mixing and mis-matching multiple prints is a high fashion approach to interior decoration but even this eclectic look needs some boundaries. The sitting room above, for example, juxtaposes a large, super-bold floral rug with an expanse of super-bold floral paper to create a vibrant, on-trend pattern clash but the fact that both prints share a common tone means that even this room remains visually cohesive.

Co-ordination may appear to be an easier look to achieve than pattern clash - after all, it's just a question of filling the room with matching prints - but, unless you're looking to recreate the 1980s, you need to think very carefully about how you furnish the space: rooms sporting co-ordinated floral patterns are no place for fussy furniture. Go instead for simple shapes and plain, pale colours. In the home-office above, for example, basic white shelving and furniture keeps the room looking fresh, light and modern despite the traditional chintzy wallpaper.

This room with its matching curtains and tablecloth is full of retro Eighties references. It's a witty look for serious pattern-lovers and the fact that it stays the right side of nostalgic pastiche is entirely down to the furniture: light, sculptural and highly contemporary, it acts as a striking contrast to the dark tones and intense busyness of the walls. The three transparent chairs are particularly effective, as they give the room an unmistakably modern edge whilst appearing to take up no space at all.

JOSEF FRANK (1885-1967)

Josef Frank trained as an architect, emerging in the 1900s – along with Otto Wagner, Josef Hoffmann and Adolf Loos – as one of the leading forces of Viennese Modernism. Today, however, he is best known as the founder of Swedish Modernism, an altogether more comfortable and easy-to-live-with take on the style. It's a title he claimed for himself: when asked to comment on his contribution to the Swedish design scene he replied, 'I have saved Swedish design in its entirety and created Scandinavian style.'

The break with functional Viennese Modernism came in the 1920s when Frank began to develop his own aesthetic, one which concentrated on humanity, congeniality, elegance and colour.

'A home should be restful to the eyes and revive the senses,' he said. 'There is no room for puritanical principles in good interior design.'

By the 1930s, Frank had all but abandoned architecture in favour of furniture, interior design and the joyous, vividly coloured textiles for which he is now best remembered.

A fan of William Morris, Frank was inspired by the natural world. His informal and highly decorative designs caught the attention of Estrid Ericson, co-founder of Swedish interior design company Svenskt Tenn. Initially commissioned to design furniture for the Company, in 1934 (having emigrated to Sweden to escape the rise of Nazism) he was appointed Svenskt Tenn's chief designer. It was the start of an artistic collaboration that was to last until his death 33 years later.

Frank produced 160 textile designs for Svenskt Tenn, all painted in watercolour. In 1947, responding to the post-war fashion for patterned walls, he produced collection of 10 wallpapers printed with his trademark, real-meets-surreal florals. These papers were radical both in their use of colour and in the intensity of the print, and they ran completely counter to the sternly plain functionalism that was fashionable at the time. But the general public loved them. 'His designs were unique, timeless, organic and warm,' says Lisa Wikfeldt of Svenskt Tenn.

In this living room, a cool, monochrome palette acts as a visual anchor for the three contrasting floral prints.

The rooms on these pages may, at first glance, look as if the designers behind them threw away
the decorating rule book but, in fact, they both adhere to two basic pattern-calming principles:
allow one pattern to dominate and stick to a colour scheme. The delicate, scrolling foliage print
in the foreground of the room above, for example, picks out the background shade of the over-
sized floral paper on the back wall and also acts as a balancing frame around the bolder design.
A lampshade, printed in an echo of the dominant wallpaper, cleverly brings the pattern into
the foreground.

The room on the left certainly lies at the extreme end of the pattern mixing spectrum but
even here there is a linking, anchor colour (yellow), while the plain white door between the two
spaces provides some visual breathing space.

Pasting all your prints onto one wall is another effective way of doing the vibrant, pattern clash thing - and since the effect is controlled by the fact that the pattern is confined to a single wall, you can afford to ignore the rule about unifying colour schemes. However, you do have to decorate the rest of the room so that the patterned wall remains the central focus. In the child's room on this page for example, the intensely patterned walls have been set against a low-key, graphic mix of white and black.

TRIAD FROM SANDERSON

These days co-ordinated pattern books, with their in-situ photographs of perfectly matched fabrics and wallpapers, are so commonplace that it's hard to believe there was ever a time before. But in 1961 off-the-peg co-ordination was hard to find. By the end of 1962, however, matching fabric and wallpaper collections were coming to be seen as the only way forward for companies aiming at the middle mass market. And it was all thanks to Triad.

Launched by the Perivale Wallpaper Division of British interior textile company Arthur Sanderson & Sons Ltd, Triad contained 68 matching wallpapers and fabrics. Each design consisted of two wallpapers and one fabric (hence the collection's title). These hand-printed papers, with their small repeat floral patterns, were as easy on the eye as they were on the wallet and success was instant: Triad became the biggest and fastest selling wallpaper collection in Britain, changing both the way people decorated and Sanderson's financial fortunes. It was popular in the rest of the world too, selling particularly well in Australia, New Zealand, Canada and South Africa. 'Triad was the beginning of commercial interior co-ordination for the masses,' says Sanderson's ex-Managing Director and former Design Director Michael Parry.

Triad is now known as Options and, while it's no longer the runaway best seller it was, the idea of affordably priced, easy to live with, ready-matched floral schemes remains popular amongst consumers across the world.

ZONING

Open-plan living has become the model for contemporary interiors but, all too often, multi-functional areas lack focus and intimacy and, once we've swept up the dust created by knocking out all our internal walls, we're left wondering how precisely to inhabit these new, free-range living spaces. The chicest solution to the problem is to create zones. Furniture, rugs and screens are all useful zoning tools but the easiest and most effective way to create a room-within-a-room is to cover a single wall with wallpaper.

Corners and alcoves are tailor-made for wallpaper zoning, enabling you to create cosy, private spaces within multi-purpose rooms. However, as the pictures on these two pages prove, papering a single wall can be just as effective. In the room on the right, for example, the owners have used a partition wall to create separate living and eating spaces. Papering this wall further emphasises the separateness of the two areas but, because the paper in the living section picks out the pink tones of the paper in the dining area, it also provides a subtle visual link between the two.

In the space above, a dramatic black wallpaper has been used to mark out the sitting area. The change from white to black signals a shift of mood and pace – the white zone is for eating and working, this black zone is all about cosy relaxation. The floral print also brings a bit of comforting softness to this otherwise rather stern and masculine room.

FEATURE WALLS

Modern floral wallpaper is extravagant stuff and while running it wall-to-wall and teaming it with mis-matched carpets and curtains is said to be the look of the future it's not one that's particularly easy to live with. The single (or even, as demonstrated the dining space above, double) feature wall however works every time. Choose the dominant wall in the room (that's the one you see first as you go in) and team with paint or a plain paper in a toning shade for maximum subtlety or meet the pattern mix thing half way by painting the remaining walls in a solid, clashing colour. Whichever option you choose, remember this is all about making the paper stand out so keep the furniture and furnishings low-key.

NEISHA CROSLAND

'People like the familiarity of floral wallpaper,' says British designer Neisha Crosland, 'and because, pattern-wise, there are lots of things that you can extract from flowers, they have been a continual source of inspiration for designers and artists.'

Crosland herself, who has been designing wallpaper ever since interior textile company Osborne & Little commissioned a collection based on her graduate show back in 1986, likes to extract all but the bare essentials. This is partly due to cost – each colour used on a paper has a dedicated roller costing around £800 so limiting the colours is an economic necessity – but also to her natural inclination towards simplicity. 'When I first saw fabrics from the Ottoman Empire I was struck by their simple, bold starkness,' she explains, 'and I have been trying to strip back my designs ever since.'

Simple they may be but Crosland's papers are also joyously patterned, designed to flow around all four walls of a room (a decorating idea which has been out of favour since the 1970s but one which she is convinced is due a major come back). And consumers love them. Neisha Crosland wallpaper now sells in 16 countries across the world with 'Birdtree' and 'Anemone' consistenty topping the sales charts. The appeal of Crosland's designs can be attributed to two things: her attention to repeat, scale and proportion which gives them a soothing, rhythmic quality that's easy to live with and the feel-good familiarity of those floral motifs.

FLORENCE BROADHURST (1899–1977)

Florence Broadhurst was nothing if not flamboyant. A talented self-publicist – some would even say fantasist (she insisted, for example, that she was a blue-blooded Brit when in fact she was born in rural Queensland) – there is some doubt as to whether or not she actually designed any of the 530 'Florence Broadhurst' papers herself as her eyesight was very poor. But no matter; she was without question the creative force behind the brand and the papers produced under its name revolutionised Australia's decorative tastes during the 1960s and 1970s.

Broadhurst came late to wallpaper design (earlier careers included singing vaudeville, running a couture fashion house and managing a trucking business), opening her studio in 1959 at the age of 60. Wallpaper was hot news in America and Europe at this time but it had yet to take off in Australia and Broadhurst believed it was her mission to introduce this rather conservative nation to bold pattern and hot, vibrant colour combinations. (Think fuchsia pink with lemon yellow and lime green with vivid orange.)

It's difficult to categorise Broadhurst's designs: colour and pattern are her hallmarks but she embraced all genres from whimsical pictures of animals to abstract graphics and exotic florals. She was technologically diverse too; on the one hand she was hugely excited by the new high-tech metallic papers that were starting to appear in America and began importing Mylar (a washable, mirror-surfaced paper) for her own designs, while on the other she blended her own colours using an old food mixer and insisted on hand screen printing every paper the factory produced.

The results were both beautiful and extraordinary and by the mid 1970s Florence Broadhurst had cornered the top end of the Australian wallpaper market. However, her brutal – and still unsolved – murder at the Sydney studio in 1977 brought the business to an abrupt end.

But only for a decade. Fortunately, Australian wallpaper company Signature Prints came across the archive, recognised its potential and, in 1989, began re-issuing Broadhurst's designs. Today the papers are distributed across the world where they are exciting a whole new generation. As David Lennie, CEO of Signature Prints says, 'Florence Broadhurst's papers are superbly designed, opulent in scale and feature clever and fashionable colourations. And they're full of her passion for experimentation too.'

Wild prints were made for feature walls. In the picture below, the vividly coloured and intensely patterned paper on the partition wall is obviously the central feature of the room and everything else simply a supporting backdrop. However, traditional small-scale spriggy florals can also become the main decorative event - it's just a question of giving them space to show off. Take your lead from the image above and limit visual competition to a couple of simple pieces.

WALL-TO-WALL PRINTS

Low-ceilinged basements are not the ideal places for large-scale, wrap-around floral prints but, as this floral strewn basement proves, anything can be made to succeed if it's done with sufficient confidence.

So why does this space work? Firstly, the paper has been used on a grand enough scale. To have confined it to a single wall would have both lessened its impact and made it appear fussy, which would have had the effect of closing the room down. Secondly, it has been allowed to take centre stage. The stone floor and simple dining furniture make ideal neutral backdrops, while the pictures highlight the background tones of the paper. And thirdly, there's that multi-coloured floral chair, providing an essential note of mis-matched chic.

PLAYING WITH SCALE

Traditionally, decorating rules have stated that large patterns should only be used in large rooms, but dare to turn this dictate on its head and you discover that large patterns can in fact look rather fabulous in small rooms too. Yes, papering a small room in an outsize print will emphasise its diminutive proportions but it will also fill the room with character, which a coat of supposedly space-enhancing white paint will not.

But you don't have to have a small room to play with scale. The owners of the spacious dining room in the image on the right, for example, have managed to achieve the large print-small space look by enclosing their paper within individual wall panels. The effect is further enhanced by the juxtaposition of over-sized objects such as the vase with the small-scale pattern on the parquet floor.

DESIGNERS GUILD

British design house Designer's Guild was born out of frustration. 'There were lots of wonderful interior designers in London in the 1960s but there was no interior design lifestyle for consumers to buy into,' explains the Company's Founder and Creative Director Tricia Guild. 'I simply couldn't find the inspiring fabrics that I wanted to work with so I decided to start designing my own. I began by re-colouring some hand-blocked textiles but I soon realised that consumers didn't know how to use them so I decided to open a small shop on London's Kings Road.'

That was back in the early Seventies. Today the shop is still there and it's still filled with the vibrantly coloured and surprisingly versatile prints that have become Tricia Guild's trademark but it's all on a much bigger scale. For example, the shop now occupies 66,000 feet of prime retail space, the distribution network now covers over 60 counties and the product range now contains more than 3,000 fabrics and 2,000 wallpapers.

Wallpaper wasn't part of the original business plan but Guild soon realised that the seventies home decorator had a real appetite for papered walls. The first floral paper, Poppy Vase, was launched in 1977 and was an instant hit, quickly establishing florals as key component of the Designer's Guild look.

'Flowers form a crucial part of my creative process, providing inspiration for patterns and colours,' Guild explains. 'They mix well with all our other decorative designs too – the plains, geometrics and stripes.'

And it is Guild's talent for demonstrating that versatility that has enabled her to turn a small fabric boutique into an international design emporium.

FERM LIVING

Not many people decide to start their own businesses based
on the insights of a clairvoyant, but for Danish graphic designer
Trine Anderson being told that she should go it alone and pursue
her passion for graphic design, interiors and fashion was just the
push she needed. So she resigned from her job and, in 2005,
Ferm Living was born. The business began as a graphic design
agency, expanding into wallpaper a year later after Anderson's
unsuccessful attempts to find any paper she liked enough to use in
her own home.

Anderson has a talent for re-interpreting retro designs in clean
and modern ways. Her papers are inspired chiefly by the natural
world, 'There is nothing more simple and more complex than
elements from nature,' she says – but they are far from chintzy
sprigs. These are flowers at their simplest and most graphic –
think winter trees, silhouettes of leaves and linear repeats of berry-
tipped branches.

Designed to be used as decoration on a single wall or as focal
points on stairs, doors and lamps, these wallpapers are selling to
fans of minimal – and distinctly Scandinavian – prettiness all over
the world.

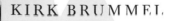

KIRK BRUMMEL

American wallpaper company Kirk Brummel was launched in 1966 by Michael Brummel and Richard Kirkham. It started out producing technically innovative, hand-printed paper that reflected both the Modern Art Movement at the time and Brummel's personal love of the Wiener Werkstätte and Art Moderne. (He trained at architecture and design school then studied for a time in Vienna.)

But as well as these rather graphic, linear papers, the company was also commissioning what Brummel describes as 'really lush things' by exciting young designers, including Billy McCarty Cooper. Cooper was one of Sixties London's most celebrated interior designers (he designed drawing rooms for the Rothschilds and Vidal Sassoon salons in Beverly Hills) and his work for Kirk Brummel was nothing if not extravagant. The Luxuriants Collection, for example, featured huge, vividly coloured, exotic floral prints that were a real departure from the cool, abstract papers which dominated the company's output at the time. But they chimed perfectly with contemporary tastes and during the 1970s Kirk Brummel expanded across America and into Europe.

Today the company is a division of wallpaper and textile company Brunschwig and Fils but its designs remain firmly linked to Kirk Brummel's heritage. Everything is still printed by hand ('Hand printing gives a wonderful depth of colour,' explains Michael Brummel, 'and the slight irregularities it creates are all part of the art form') and, in 2007, Brummel took the decision to re-launch some of Cooper's Luxuriant designs.

'I think we are seeing a wonderful return to a little more voluptuousness in form,' he explains, 'and these designs are certainly voluptuous.'

The right wallpaper can turn even the most utilitarian room into a thing of beauty. This bathroom had to be adapted for wheelchair use, but the owner was determined not to let the functional fittings dominate so she papered the walls in this large-scale – and slightly surreal – lily print. Extending the paper onto the landing outside makes both spaces appear bigger.

OTHER USES

Wallpaper isn't only for walls – in fact, the first single sheet papers were used to decorate chests and boxes rather than entire rooms. Today, thanks to the ready availability of large rolls of wallpaper, we can think on a grander scale but we should still be inspired by the idea of papering furniture.

'Wallpapering is the best way to turn old or boring furniture into something eye-poppingly chic,' says interior designer and craft queen Danielle Proud. And it's not that difficult, as her six-step guide to papering a chest of drawers proves.

1. Remove all knobs and handles, then sand the entire surface and wipe clean with a damp cloth.

2. Take the drawers out in order and number each one so you can put them back correctly.

3. Keeping the drawers in order, place them face down on the back of your wallpaper, making sure the pattern is the right way up. Position the drawers exactly as they are when in the chest of drawers, draw around each one, making a note of the number on the back of the wallpaper.

4. Paint the rest of the chest in a paint colour matched to the background colour of the wallpaper – this saves having to paper every last nook, curve and cranny.

5. Cut out the drawer shapes using a craft knife and metal ruler, then stick each to the corresponding drawer front using roll-on craft glue or wallpaper paste. Brush over with a dry wallpaper brush to ensure there are no bubbles or pockets of glue under the surface. Wipe away any excess glue.

6. Leave to dry overnight then seal with four or five coats of clear, acrylic sealant.

And it's not just the outsides of furniture that can benefit from decoration: papering the inside of cupboards is a very effective way of adding interest to otherwise dead spaces. Turn glass-fronted cupboards into functional art works by lining them in your favourite print or go for the element of surprise and decorate the inside of a solid cupboard.

Wallpaper can also be used to turn overlooked areas such as landings, halls, stairways and cloakrooms into striking feature rooms in their own right – and as these spaces are transitory and largely unfurnished you can afford to be really bold. There's no limit to the possibilities but here are four to try:

1. Disguise functional hallway cupboards with a length of panoramic paper. Covering the inside of the doors in a contrasting paper will create an added visual surprise.

2. Transform small halls or cloakrooms into glamorous treasure boxes by papering both the walls and ceiling in a richly patterned paper.

3. Celebrate long thin landings by running a geometric print along both walls.

4. Lining a stairway wall in an over-sized floral print will add a sense of drama to the centre of the house. (Opt for a busy design if finger marks are an issue.)

Beautiful contemporary

floral wallpapers

to brighten your life.

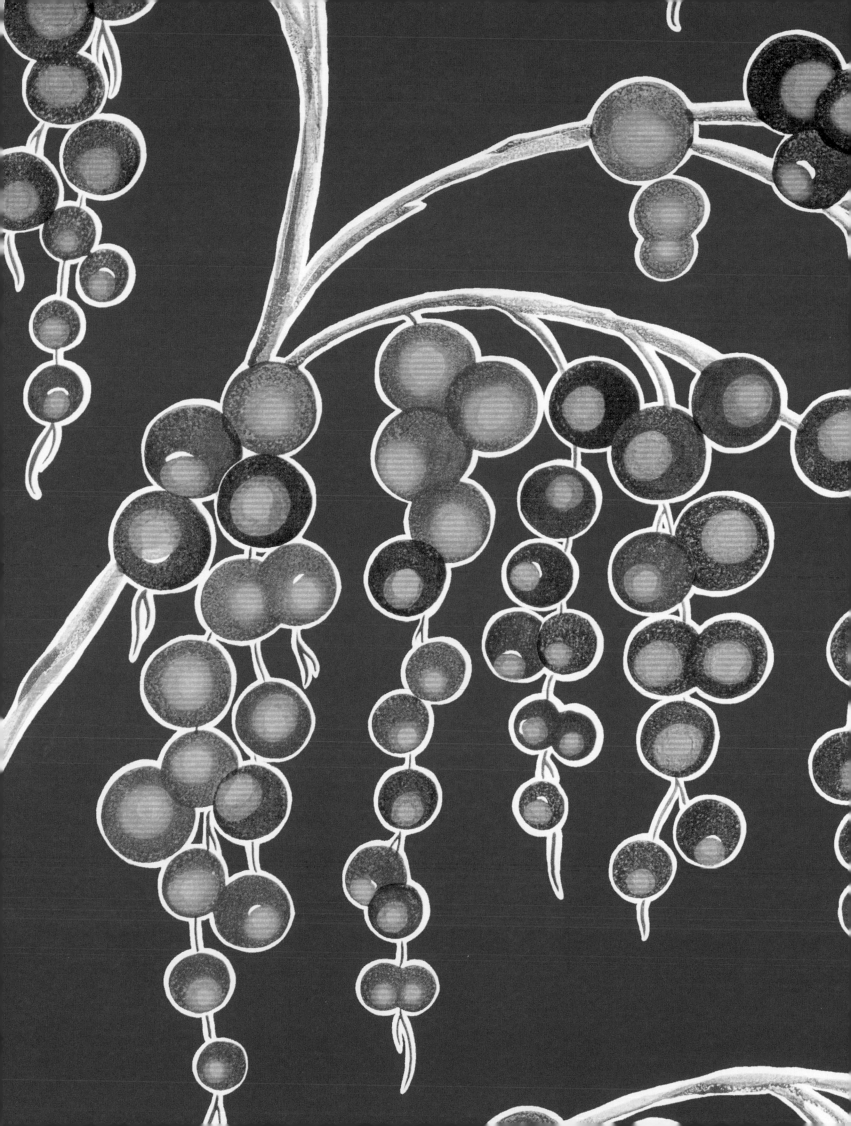

Pasted Pictures

Wallpaper designers have been using pictures to decorate their work for almost as long as they have used pattern. Styles range from the simplest still life repeats to photo-real imitations of fabric and extravagant, sweeping panoramic landscapes but what inspires them all - and explains the lasting appeal of the genre - is the desire to create an alternative world within an ordinary domestic environment.

CHINOISERIE

Vibrant, decorative and wonderfully exotic, chinoiserie first arrived in Europe in the seventeenth century, imported by the hugely successful East India Trading Company. Based on the painted silk hangings popular amongst China's wealthy elite, these papers were made specifically for export (the Chinese were skilled paper makers but wallpaper as a domestic decorative device wasn't known) and were the first wallpapers in the world to be designed with a continuous image rather than a repeat pattern. However, they were not designed to be hung as a single picture but as a series of scenes separated by strips of plain paper.

The earliest papers depicted scenes of Chinese life - farmers in the paddy fields were a common theme - but by the end of the seventeenth century these had been replaced by bird and flower designs painted on rich green and deep pink grounds.

The style took a while to establish a following but by the 1740s chinoiserie had become the wall covering of choice for the well-heeled folk of Europe and America. (It was expensive stuff - in Britain in 1769 a panel cost around 63 shillings, compared with around nine shillings for a roll of good quality flock.)

Demand was so high that genuine papers couldn't be imported fast enough so, ever on the look out for new business opportunities, British wallpaper manufacturers began to make their own. They printed the designs (by this time flowering trees and figures were the most popular motifs) from an engraved plate then applied the colour by hand. The results were pretty enough but they lacked the accuracy and subtlety of the Chinese originals.

By 1790 the craze was waning - especially in France where taste shapers were being seduced by homegrown scenic wallpaper. There was a brief revival of interest in Regency Britain, resulting in the chinoiserie extravaganza that was the Brighton Pavilion, but by 1880 chinoiserie-covered walls had become a fashion faux pas. And so they remained until the start of the twenty-first century when, bored by years of plain beige minimalism, we began to rediscover the decorative possibilities of wallpaper.

SCENIC PAPERS

Panoramic sceneries first appeared in France at the start of the nineteenth century. Conceived to challenge the popularity of English flock papers and to demonstrate the skills of French wallpaper makers, these papers depicted historic scenes, landscapes and mythological subjects and were designed to form a continuous mural around a room, uninterrupted by furniture and furnishings. They appealed chiefly to France's new emerging bourgeoisie, who regarded them as an acceptable alternative to the genuine decorated panels favoured by the aristocracy.

The first Papiers Peints Paysages were painted entirely by hand but after 1830, they were commonly block printed on a continuous roll. Even with this technological development, production remained slow and laborious since each paper required between 100 and 4,000 blocks.

Two companies dominated the scenic paper scene – and both were French: Zuber et Cie, who produced the very first Papier Peint Paysage, 'Vue de Suisse', in 1804 and Dufour et Leroy, famous for topographical papers such as 'Monuments de Paris,' which depicted the city's great buildings arranged, with some artistic licence, along the banks of the Seine. America had a small scenic industry of its own (M.H. Birge and Co opened a factory in New York in 1834 and in the 1930s there were several companies producing scenics for the home market) but its considerable appetite for panoramic papers was chiefly satisfied by the American-theme papers produced for export by Zuber et Cie. Britain and the rest of Europe largely ignored the craze (in Britain there was a brief flurry of interest in scenic papers commemorating special events such as the arrival of the first giraffe at London Zoo) considering it easier to get the look with a painted mural. Until recently that is. Today, thanks to digital printing, photo-real scenic wallpaper is easy to make and cheap to buy and is consequently set to be a major decorative trend once more.

TOILE DE JOUY

Today, toile de Jouy is a generic term for a single-coloured scenic print used on both fabric and wallpaper. Its origins, however, go back to eighteenth-century France and the Oberkampf factory at Jouy-en-Josas where engraved copper plates were used to print scenes of pastoral life and momentous historical moments (one famously shows the end of the American war of independence) onto calico fabric. Highly decorative yet easy on the eye due to the monochrome colour palette (red, blue, violet and buff were the most common colours), toile de Jouy became an instant design classic.

How and Where to Use

Pictorial wallpapers seek our attention in a way that patterned papers do not so, in some senses, they are the most demanding of all the wallpaper genres. However, they are also fantastically easy and satisfying to use; think of them as central features in their own right rather than as purely decorative backgrounds for art works and ornaments and you can't go wrong.

ZONING

If you are lucky enough to have a large open-plan living space then, as the rooms on these pages show, pictorial papers make ideal zoning tools. In the image on the right, for example, the owner has papered an alcove with a trompe l'oeil bookcase to create a cosy – and rather witty – room within a room. But you don't need an alcove to do the zoning thing. If all you have are four flat walls, take one – or a section of one – and cover it with your favourite paper. And since open-plan rooms are often chilly, do as the owners of the space above have done and go for something richly coloured that will create a sense of warmth and comfort.

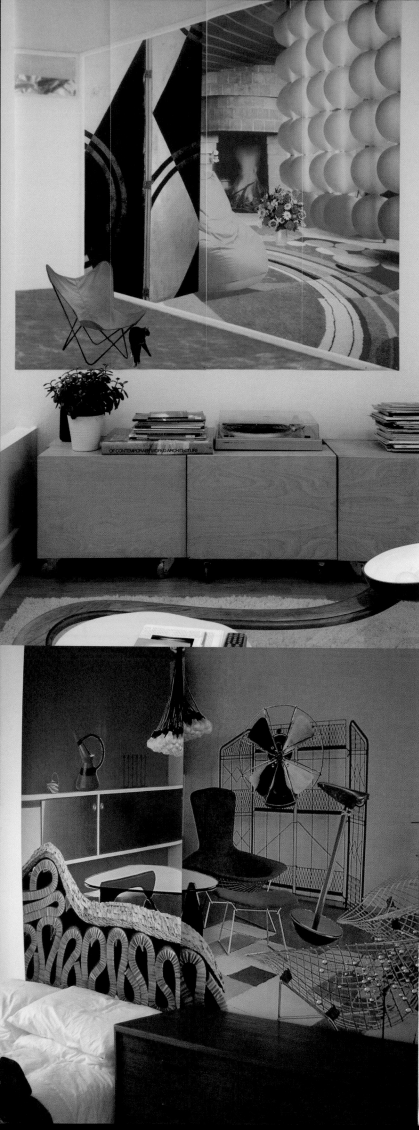

DORKENWALD-SPITZER

Sarah Dorkenwald and Ruth Spitzer have always been interested in issues surrounding mobility, adaptation and transformation. Their design company, Dorkenwald-Spitzer, founded in Toronto in 2002, was established specifically to turn these rather abstract concepts into physical products. Products such as their extraordinary, modern take on trompe l'oeil wallpaper.

The Wallfurniture collection, which is digitally printed onto lightfast, washable wallpaper fleece, features hyper-real photographs of fully furnished rooms. 'The collection has been designed with today's mobile society in mind,' Dorkenwald explains. 'The pre-printed images of furniture and accessories stand in for the real thing.'

Spitzer agrees. 'Wallfurniture creates a temporary home, a sense of well being and the feeling of being truly settled in, even if the room you have just moved into is completely empty,' she says.

Wallfurniture is also rather aspirational. These are no run-of-the-mill digital rooms; these are illusionary interiors for the design conscious. Yes, there are ordinary things such as vacuum cleaners and discarded training shoes but the key pieces are all twentieth-century design icons – think Le Corbusier's LC2 sofa, Harry Bertoia's wire chairs and Charles and Ray Eames' rocking armchair.

'As well as playing with the illusion of invented space,' Dorkenwald and Spitzer explain, 'Wallfurniture is also about creating humorous contrasts between everyday objects and design classics.'

FEATURE WALLS

Papers depicting a single image deserve to be treated as artworks rather than wallpaper. Digital printing has relaunched a trend for trompe l'oeil not seen since eighteenth-century France. British designer Deborah Bowness was one of the first to experiment with contemporary trompe l'oeil. Her work is distinctly domestic, featuring images of such prosaic pieces as standard lamps and clothes and each one is meant to be mixed with real furniture. Her 'Frocks and Hooks' paper, top left, is sold with a set of fully functioning hangers so real clothes can be hung alongside the trompe l'oeil frocks. 'The juxtaposition of a real dress with the optical illusion of a dress is odd, trippy and questioning,' she says, 'and that's the point. It's about making people jump between reality and illusion.'

ROGER NICHOLSON (1922–1986)

Roger Nicholson trained as a painter at the Royal College of Art (RCA) in London but he earned his living as a commercial designer. In 1945, he set up a graphic design partnership with his brother, Robert Nicholson – a design firm that was regarded at the time as one of the most promising in the country.

By 1958 Nicholson was Professor of Textiles at the RCA and had begun working with the hugely influential Wallpaper Manufacturers Ltd (W.P.M) – an umbrella organisation which controlled 98% of all English wallpaper manufacturing. It was a collaboration that led him to work on the ground-breaking Palladio collection of wallpapers. Produced by W.P.M members Lightbown & Aspinall and Sanderson, the Palladio papers were all designed by specially commissioned artists and were aimed primarily at architects. With their largely abstract imagery and huge pattern repeats (the papers were screen printed by hand to free the artists from the size constraints imposed by machine printing), these were papers for the brave and were mainly used in commercial and public buildings but they had a huge impact on tastes of the time.

Nicholson might not have made his name as a fine artist but the commercial work that made him famous reflected his painter's eye. Michael Parry, former Managing Director of Sanderson says, 'Nicholson painted his observations on everyday life with an efficiency, clarity and authority in everything he saw.' His pictorial papers demonstrate this perfectly. 'Hopscotch' and 'Locomotion', for example, which he designed in 1955 and 1958 for Lightbown & Aspinall, are both accurate depictions of their subject matter (childhood games in the case of 'Hopscotch' and modes of transport in 'Locomotion') but the pictures are drawn with a spare simplicity and such attention to the structure of the repeat that they take on a decorative rhythm ideally suited to domestic wallpaper. As Zoë Hendon, Senior Curator of the Museum of Domestic Architecture, Middlesex University, comments, 'Roger Nicholson's pictorial wallpaper designs have a playful and charming simplicity and a lightness of touch which gives them an appealing freshness even today.'

Tracy Kendall also specialises in designing wallpaper that plays visual tricks. This paper was printed from a digital photograph of the actual plates stacked on the shelf beside it, causing the onlooker to question what is reality and what is illusion. On a more practical level, hanging the paper next to the shelves also creates a sense of space because it appears to double the size of the shelf unit.

CONTEMPORARY PANORAMICS

Panoramic papers are designed to form continuous scenes, either across a single wall or right around the room. First popular in France and America in the nineteenth century they are now experiencing a revival, thanks to digital technology and our increasing willingness to take a bold approach to interior decoration.

The most cutting-edge twenty-first-century panoramics are all about reality. Cityscapes such as the one in the kitchen shown here, bottom far right, and scenes of everyday interiors dominate the high-fashion end of the style, appealing to a cosmopolitan, urban audience too well-travelled to delight in the exotic landscapes which characterised the genre first time around.

There are plenty of exceptions to the trend of course. Companies such as Zuber et Cie and US-based Gracie, are reproducing classic panoramics and ornate chinoiseries (which, as the picture above shows, can look utterly contemporary when set against spare, modern furniture), while others specialise in providing kitsch, hyper-real images such as Surface View's 'Lady of the Orient', top right, for consumers keen to revive the 1970s craze for giant photo murals.

And there are lots of modern versions of fantasy landscape-style panoramics too. Sun dappled forests, elegant tree-lined avenues, woodland waterfalls – there's a scene to suit everyone and all it takes to transform your room is some wallpaper paste and a meticulous eye for detail. (Let your mind wander and you'll get the running order of the rolls mixed up which will leave you with a disjointed scene.)

Designer Martine Aballea created this extraordinary forest-scape, above, from a photograph which she reworked on a computer and then treated with paper paint so that it covers her bedroom wall like a fresco.

Panoramic wallpapers allow you to play games with perspective and proportions – a landscape image such as the avenue of trees above, for example, appears to draw you on past the walls into the scene beyond. This makes them perfectly suited to small, viewless spaces such as hallways, landings, cloakrooms and bathrooms. When it comes to the furnishings, try and keep everything below eye level so as not to spoil the view and remember less is almost always more. (The busily furnished sitting-cum-dining room, above right, is an exception to the rule and it works because the owners have stuck to a predominantly green palette.)

Panoramic papers don't have to be as visually demanding as those shown on the previous pages. The one on the left, for example, with its simple, almost repeating tree print and gentle sepia tones is discreet and soothing, while the world map, above, takes on an abstract pattern-like appearance when used on this scale.

The owners of both interiors have also echoed the dominant tone of their chosen wallpaper in the rest of the room (soft browns in the bedroom, cool blues in the sitting room), ensuring that the overall effect is subtle and low-key.

FROMENTAL

'The great thing about chinoiserie,' says Tim Butcher, one half of British handmade wallpaper company Fromental, 'is its grand old age. It has this fantastic heritage and it's so beautiful and timeless that it will fit with any architecture.'

And he should know – before launching Fromental in 2005 along with his wife Lizzie Deshayes and their Financial Director Dave Jones, Butcher was Creative Director of the world's leading chinoiserie house de Gournay.

Not that chinoiserie had been the original intention. 'When we first started the company,' Deshayes remembers, 'we proposed designs that were much more modern: the Chinoiserie Collection came about by popular demand.'

It may be inspired by the grandeur of traditional eighteenth-century designs but Fromental's take on chinoiserie is unusual and thoroughly contemporary. The breakthrough came when Butcher, who had previously worked in fashion, decided to try embroidering paper. The first design he produced featured strands of silk twined together and hand-stitched onto a silk background. It was elegant, beautiful and completely unique so he decided to try hand-stitching over their chinoiserie too. 'We couldn't believe that these two ancient traditions hadn't been combined before,' says Deshayes. 'We've never looked back and neither have our clients.'

Fromental's papers, which are all designed by them in their London studio, are made entirely by hand in workshops North East of Shanghai. They are painted and embroidered on silk which is then backed onto paper made (also by hand) from the pulped bark of Mulberry trees. It is a painstaking process – one panel can take over 150 hours to produce – so this is not wallpaper as mere decoration: this is wallpaper as wall couture. So how are people using it? 'Traditionally, chinoiserie papers were used in bedrooms, drawing and dining rooms,' explains Butcher, 'but we have found that people also like to use them in unexpected places such as staircases, hallways and even kitchens. Luckily, with modern paints and finishes we can make them durable in these more challenging areas without compromising their delicate effect.'

And what about the great feature wall versus full room debate? Deshayes and Butcher are adamant in their reply. 'Wallpaper only really comes to life when it wraps around a room. It's about bringing a sense of magic in 360 degrees.'

CHILDREN'S ROOMS

Pictorial designs have been used to decorate children's rooms since the 1870s. The original idea was that these papers should educate and improve impressionable young minds so depictions of historical events and images of perfectly behaved children engaged in wholesome play were the most common themes.

Today wallpaper as educator and moraliser has given way to wallpaper as decorative entertainment (although alphabet friezes still have a firm following) and, while football and TV themes seem to dominate the mass market, beautifully drawn pictorial papers, such as the flamingos seen here, can still be found.

Children's bedrooms are generally cluttered places so busy pictorial papers should be used with care - after all, too much visual stimulation isn't conducive to a quiet night. In this room the paper has been mixed with plenty of calming white furniture.

TRADITIONAL PANORAMICS

Inspired by a collection of nineteenth-century lithographs and drawings, de Gournay's traditional-style panoramic paper, 'North American River Views', was designed in 2006 by the company's in-house team and New York-based interior designer Thomas Jayne. It is an epic scene, depicting the southern flatlands of the Mississippi Delta, with its plantation houses and paddle steamers, as well as the Hudson River and mountainous landscapes surrounding the Niagara Falls. It has been used in domestic (albeit grand) dining rooms and entrance halls around the world.

These panoramic papers are all made to order, hand-painted panel by panel by artists who follow a precise pattern to ensure the picture flows seamlessly. It's a specialist, time-consuming process, which means the papers don't come cheap. So, if you are investing in a panoramic such as this, it's worth doing as nineteenth-century fans of the style did and mounting it on boards rather than pasting it straight on to the wall so that you can take it with you when you move.

ZUBER ET CIE

The world's first panoramic wallpaper was produced by French company Zuber et Cie in 1804. Designed by leading artist Pierre Mongon, 'Vues de Suisse', as this ground-breaking paper was called, did away with the traditional repeat pattern and instead gave people a continuous, panoramic landscape that was intended to transform rooms and spirit the viewer away to an idealised foreign land.

Zuber et Cie had already made a name for itself as a manufacturer of trompe l'oeil wallpapers (its 'drapery' friezes, for example, were in high demand) but scenic wallpapers such as 'Vues de Suisse' were new and – in France at least – they became instantly fashionable amongst the wealthy.

Zuber et Cie was not the only French company to make Papiers Peints Paysages (as these panoramic papers were called) but it did lead the way, both in terms of design and technical expertise. In the early 1900s, for example, it developed a special hand brush painting technique known as Irisé which merged shades seamlessly to create subtle and realistic skyscapes. And skyscapes were important – in most designs over half the paper was given over to the sky so that the papers could be trimmed to size without affecting the main scene.

Making these papers was a painstaking process. First, the entire roll of paper was painted by hand using the Irisé technique. The design was then printed on top of this base coat using wooden blocks. Each colour required a different block and these papers were colourful creations: Deltil's 'Vues d'Amerique du Nord', for example, featured 233 different shades. The blocks themselves were so intricately carved that it often took as many as 20 engravers an entire year to prepare the blocks needed for a single scene. No wonder then that panoramics only sold to the super wealthy and that in the 50 or so years of their high-fashion status Zuber only produced 25 different scenes.

The market for these papers today is small – price aside, few people have the space for wallpaper on such epic scale – but the French scenic papers pioneered by Zuber et Cie are a fascinating moment in the story of interior decoration.

CHINOISERIE

Tim Butcher and Lizzie Deshayes, the husband and wife team behind handmade wallpaper design studio Fromental, have used their own extravagant chinoiserie paper in their sitting room, combining it with pattern-rich soft furnishings.

'I don't think wallpaper should be used in a precious way,' says Lizzie Deshayes. 'It's just a wall treatment after all. Historically, chinoiserie wallpapers were in rooms used for entertaining and showing off because it looks terrific with the most ornate furniture. Chinoiserie almost demands to be next to other busy patterns rather than in splendid isolation. It's a minimalist's worst nightmare.'

GRACIE

Founded in Manhattan in 1898 by Charles R. Gracie, Gracie has been selling high quality, hand-painted chinoiserie wallpaper for over a century. Mr Gracie the First (the firm is now run by his great, great grandson Mike Gracie) started out importing and selling oriental furniture, screens and porcelains.

The wallpaper business started almost by chance when, in the late 1920s, a textile trader friend of Charles Gracie returned from Beijing with a roll of hand-painted wallpaper. Gracie thought it exquisite and decided that there was a market for these papers in the States. So, despite the Great Depression and the fact that chinoiserie had been out of fashion since the early nineteenth century, Gracie established a workshop in China and began to import.

'My great great grandfather was largely responsible for bringing chinoiserie back in the twentieth century,' says Mike Gracie. 'He was a bit of a wheeler-dealer and could sell anything if he was convinced of its beauty and quality.'

Many of America's leading interior designers, including Macmillan and Elsie de Wolfe, were equally convinced, seeing these opulent papers as the perfect antidote to the austere times. But, despite such high profile support, business continued to be tough: World War II made importing from China almost impossible and then the Chinese Revolution meant that the studio – whose management were Nationalists – had to flee to Taiwan.

Gracie's survival can be put down to determination and the lack of competition. 'Until very recently', explains Mike Gracie, 'it has been incredibly difficult to establish business in China so we were the only company producing chinoiserie at this level. Things are changing a bit now though.'

The company's response to the emerging competition has been to trade on its history (many new clients, including Estée Lauder's granddaughter, are the descendants of previous customers) and to innovate. All the papers are still hand-painted in China but the colours have been completely updated. Their best-selling design, the catchily titled 'SY206' for example, is printed on a silver leaf background.

'It's all about combining ancient techniques with a modern palette to create a really transitional product line,' Gracie explains. 'And no one else is doing that at this level.'

CELIA BIRTWELL

Celia Birtwell was one of the most fashion forward textile designers of the 1960s. The delicate, whimsical designs she produced for her then husband, fashion designer Ossie Clark, were worn by the decade's hottest names from Twiggy to Marianne Faithfull.

In 1984 Birtwell turned her attention to interiors, transferring her brand of witty, hand-painted prints onto furnishing fabrics. The minimal Nineties was a tough decade for anyone working with colour and pattern but the return of decoration in the mid-Noughties, coupled with the spectacular success of her clothing collection for high street brand Top Shop, re-established Birtwell as one of Britain's leading print designers.

Her first wallpaper collection was launched in 2006, at the request of her customers. Featuring two designs – 'Jacobean', a dynamic, all-over pattern of leaves, branches and flowers, and 'Beasties', a repeat print of appealing mythological creatures – the collection was inspired by seventeenth-century antique textiles. These are unashamedly nostalgic papers and the traditional surface printing techniques used to produce them ensure that the charming, hand-painted quality of the designs has not been lost.

Both Jacobean and Beasties were instant hits and can now be found in both drawing rooms and downstairs loos around the world. (Her clients include artist David Hockney and presenter Jonathan Ross.) Asked why Birtwell is clear: 'People are finally moving away from the safe world of plains and are starting to experiment. Pictorial papers are a nod to the past and make a rather fitting juxtaposition to the modern, technical world that we live in today.'

MIXING PICTORIAL PAPERS

With its monochrome colour palette and gentle, pastoral imagery, toile de Jouy is one of the few pictorial papers that can be used both as a central feature and as a backdrop for pictures, furniture and ornaments.

As the room above left shows, used on a grand scale and combined with matching curtains, it takes on the rhythm of a repeating pattern. Wall-to-wall toile is, of course, perfectly suited to the grandeur of this French manor house but it's a look that would work equally well in an ordinary bedroom – so long as you follow the guidelines for using wall-to-wall pattern and stick to a single, unifying colour scheme.

Chinoiserie papers also work well combined with other patterns. The repeat in the pretty chinoiserie-inspired print seen in the image above, for example, gives the paper a gentle rhythm which means it can be easily mixed with other patterns in similar tones.

Papering the wardrobe doors turns functional storage into a decorative feature and is a particularly effective way of bringing pattern into small spaces.

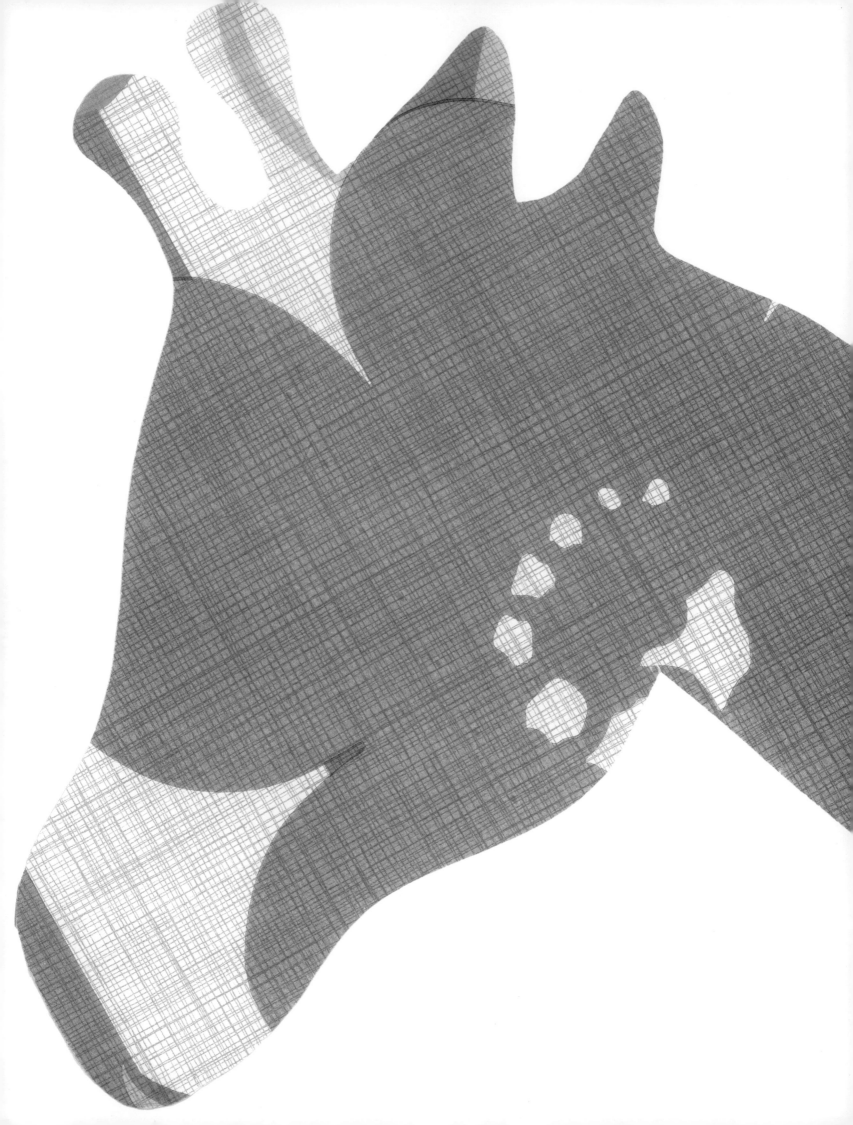

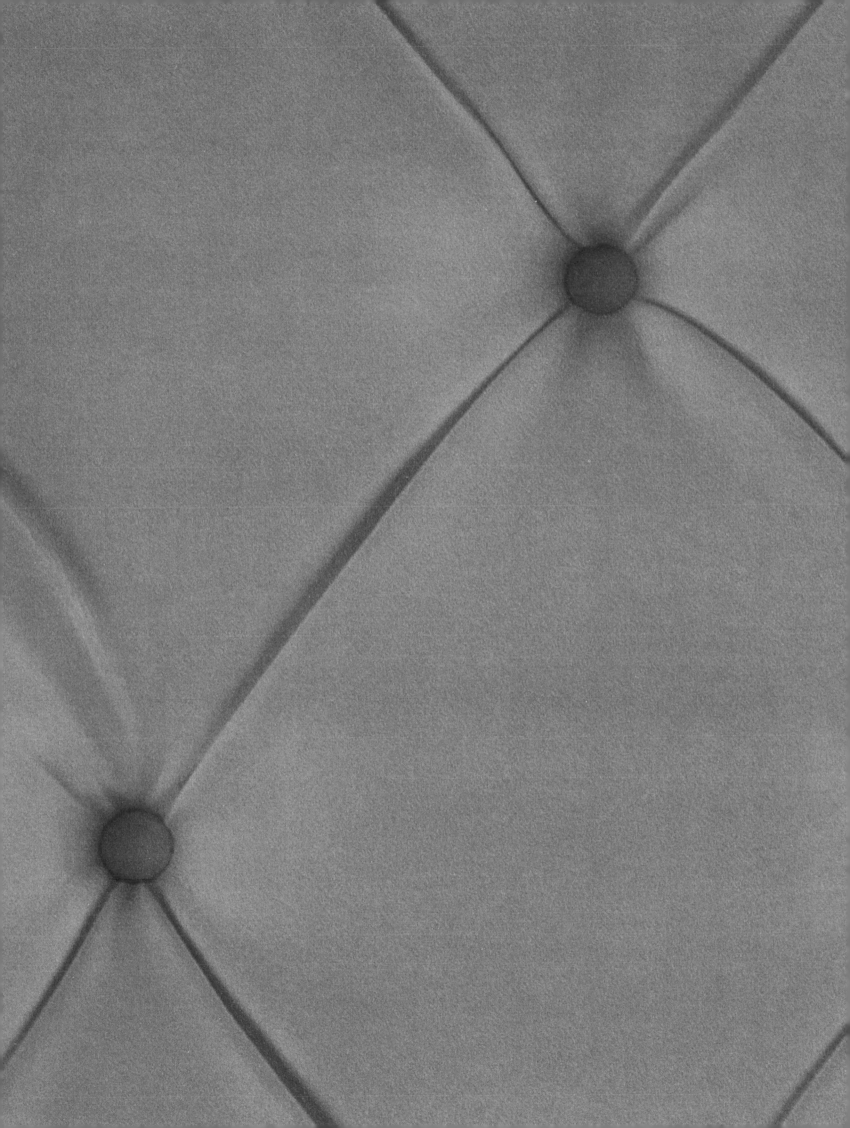

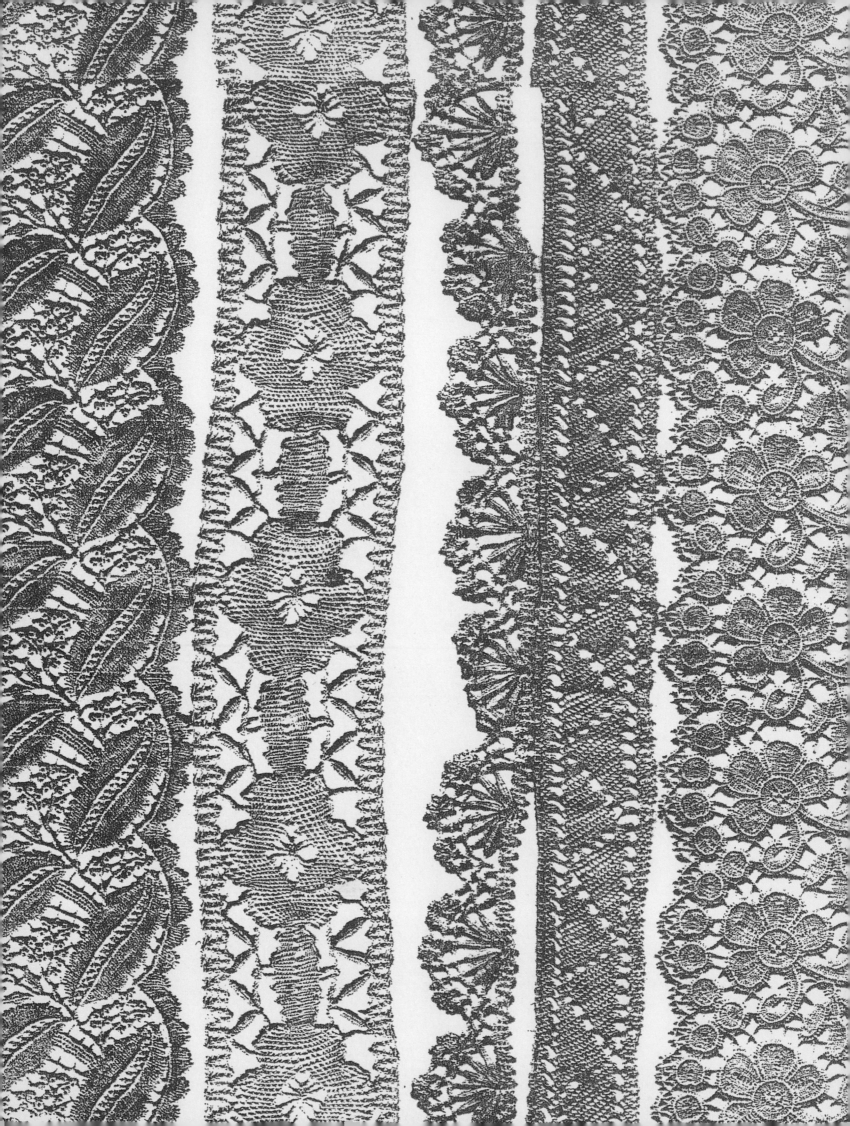

Practicalities

Essential Equipment

Stepladder
Stripping knife
Large, sharp scissors or
    trimming knife
Pasting table
Metal ruler or tape measure
Plumb line (you can make
    one using fine string with
    a weight attached to it)
Bucket with a string tied
    across the middle (this
    will help remove excess
    paste from the brush and
    keep your brush clean
    when it's not in use)
Seam roller
Pasting brush
Good quality wallpaper
    hanger's brush
Lambs wool roller
Pencil
Sponge

first piece   matching the pattern

100mm trim
allowance

length required

Measuring Up

Before you begin, you have to work out how much paper you're going to need. It's vital that you get this right: over-estimate and you're left with unused rolls but underestimate and, since wallpaper is printed in batches and colour matches are not guaranteed from batch to batch, you run the risk of ending up with slightly mis-matched walls. When measuring always use a metal tape measure. When ordering your paper, make sure all the rolls have the same batch number.

TIP: *Take your measurements with you when you go shopping and ask the supplier to double check your calculations.*

1. Measure the height of each wall from skirting board to ceiling in several places around the room. Add 100mm to the longest measurement to allow for trimming.

2. Measure the length of each wall you are planning to paper and add these measurements together.

3. Calculate the size of the area you need to paper by multiplying the wall height by the total wall length

4. Patterns have to continue above and below windows so measure them as if they were walls.

REMEMBER: *Wallpaper should be cut rather than folded into every corner so you will need a new drop for every turn.*

Repeats

If you're using patterned paper, you will also have to allow for the repeat. This is the distance between one point on the pattern to the identical point further down – the size of the repeat should be printed on the wallpaper's label. To calculate how much paper you need, follow steps 1–3 above, and then add the repeat measurement to every drop length.

Once you've bought your paper, you need to work out how the repeat will work when the paper is hung. The easiest way to do this is to open a couple of packs of paper, roll out (but don't cut) a 2m length from each and then slide the two pieces next to each other until the patterns match right across the design. You are aiming to replicate this on the wall.

Hanging

1. Preparation is everything. Walls must be clean, dry and free from bumps and holes before you apply wallpaper.

2. Lining paper is essential – it makes a good wall perfect and provides a consistent surface for the adhesive so that everything dries at the same rate. Hang it horizontally to ensure that the edge of the lining paper doesn't match the edge of the wallpaper drop. (On very long runs however, you may be better off hanging lining paper vertically as horizontal lining paper can start to crease, especially if the wall isn't perfectly plastered. In this case, simply start the wallpaper 3cm away from the lining paper start line.) Leave the lining paper to dry thoroughly (this can take up to 12 hours) before putting up your wallpaper.

TIP: *If you're using a dark wallpaper, give the lining paper a couple of coats of black paint to avoid stripes of white showing between the drops.*

3. Measure the wall that is to be papered from ceiling to skirting board. Unroll the paper on to a pasting table, right side down and draw a straight line across the paper at the measured point. Cut along this line with sharp wallpaper scissors.

4. Turn the cut length over, unroll the next length and place each piece edge to edge to match the pattern. Measure and cut as before. Repeat until you have several cut lengths. Don't forget to mark each one in the top corner so you know the running order.

5. Mix up the wallpaper paste according to the instructions on the packet.

TIP: *Always use the same paste for both the lining paper and the wallpaper so they pull at the wall and at each other at the same rate.*

6. Lay a cut length of paper on a clean, dry decorating table – the paper is likely to be longer than the table.

7. Paste the back of the paper, working from the middle to the outer edge. When you've pasted the stretch on the table, fold it over on itself concertina style, and continue pasting until the full length is covered.

Corners

1. Measure the distance between the edge of the last hung length and the corner in several places. Add 25mm to the largest measurement and cut a length of paper to this width, keeping the off-cut for papering the first length of the adjoining wall.

TIP: *Always cut into corners. Bending wallpaper around a corner will always leave you with air bubbles and creases. For internal (or concave) corners, cut the paper both into and at the corner.*

2. Paste and hang the paper, butting it to the previous piece as before. The 25mm overlap should stick lightly to the adjoining wall.

3. Smooth the paper into the corner with a paper-hanging brush and then press it down firmly with a seam roller.

4. Measure the width of the off-cut and, using a plumb line, draw a vertical line down the wall that distance from the corner. This will give you a straight edge for starting the next wall.

5. Hang the off-cut so that the left-hand edge over-laps the paper turned from the previous wall and the right-hand edge aligns with your drawn line.

8. If the room has a prominent focal point such as a fireplace, then start papering here, taking care to centre any pattern over the feature you are highlighting. If there is no obvious focal point, then begin papering on a blank wall (i.e. one with no doors, windows, radiators etc) so that you can hang a full length.

9. It's vital that the first piece is straight so, using a plumb line, draw a line down the wall from ceiling to skirting board. This line should be 48cm in from the corner to allow for some overlap onto the next wall.

10. Place the right-hand side of the first piece of pasted paper against this line, leaving a 5cm overlap at the top and bottom to allow for trimming.

11. Smooth the paper down with a hanging brush, working from the centre to the outside edges.

12. Trim the paper top and bottom.

13. Continue around the room in a clockwise direction. Butt each length against the one before and repeat steps 10 and 11.

Difficult areas

Papering a flat wall is one thing, but what do you do when you come to an obstacle? Professional paper hanger Yair Meshoulam (Wallpaper Hangers, wallpaperhangers.org.uk) gives his advice on coping with sockets, switches, stairways and doorways.

Sockets and switches

The aim here is to tuck the paper behind the edges of the socket or switch.

1. Switch the power off.

TIP: *Light and power sockets are on different circuits so plug in some good work lights once you've turned off the wall lights and then you will be able to see what you are doing.*

2. Unscrew the two holding screws and leave them with the correct screwdriver on the floor close to where you're working. Cover the front and sides of the socket/switch with low-tack masking tape.

3. Take the paper over the socket/switch, fixing it to the wall above. At the bulge, press the corners of the socket/switch against the paper to dent it slightly, then carefully cut an X from the centre of the rectangle to the corners. Cut one corner slightly longer (preferably the bottom right as this is the least visible) and pull the socket/switch through the hole.

4. Cut a 2cm border all the way round to allow for the electrics and snip off any excess paper that is covering the screw holes.

5. Continue hanging the vertical drop of wallpaper beneath the socket or switch.

6. Remove the tape and screw the socket/switch back in place.

7. Leave the paper to dry before switching the power back on.

Stairways

Don't attempt to paper a stairway yourself unless you are confident balancing on ladders and boards. Paper the area just as you would an ordinary wall but remember to measure the drops at their longest length and always make your start line the longest drop in the centre of the wall.

Doorways

Doorways should be papered as if they were internal corners (see previous page). Try to cut a slightly longer diagonal line and hang the area above the door before you start the area to the side.

TIP: *Protect all door furniture by covering it with low-tack masking tape.*

Glossary of feature wallpapers

Within the chapters, every wallpaper is shown at actual size. Here each wallpaper is shown at its full width and, wherever possible, with at least one full repeat of the design. Listed are the manufacturer and designer's name where applicable, the design name and/or design code, the measurements of the roll and the measurements of the repeat of the pattern and, of course, the website details.

Lizzie Allen
'Jazz in Central Park' in Spring
Roll size: by the metre x 55cm
Repeat: 75cm
Website: lizzieallen.co.uk

Barbara Barry
for Kravet
'Chic Link Net' (W3009-81)
Roll size: 10m x 52cm
Repeat: 54cm
Website: barbarabarry.com/kravet.com

Florence Broadhurst
for Signature Prints
'Horses Stampede' (FBW/C030)
Roll size: 10m x 71cm
Repeat: 68.8cm
Website: signatureprints.com.au

Tracy Kendall
'In the White Room'
Roll size: made to order, by the sq metre
Repeat: no repeat
Website: tracykendall.com

Jocelyn Warner
'Flora' in Graphic (JWP-904)
Roll size: 10m x 52cm
Repeat: 76.2cm
Website: jocelynwarner.com

Fromental
'Funky Bamboo' in Mist
Roll size: made to order
Repeat: no repeat
Website: fromental.co.uk

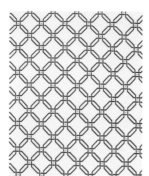

Manuel Canovas
at Colefax and Fowler
'Broadway' in Ecru/Lin
Roll size: 10m x 52cm
Repeat: 76cm
Website: manuelcanovas.com

Harlequin
'Contour' (60645) from the
Virtue Collection
Roll size: 10.5m x 52cm
Repeat: 26cm
Website: harlequin.uk.com

Manuel Canovas
at Colefax and Fowler
'Cassis' in Fuchsia (03042/04)
Roll size: 10m x 52cm
Repeat: 72cm
Website: manuelcanovas.com

Cole & Son
'Woodstock' in Orange on Gold (70/5012)
from the Classix Exotic Flock Collection
Roll size: 10m x 52cm
Repeat: 53cm (straight match)
Website: cole-and-son.com

Sally Hemphill
'Clapper'
Roll size: 10m x 51cm
Repeat: 11cm
Website: govindiahemphill.com

Élitis
'Opium' (TP 153-01-03) from the
Tenue de Soirée Collection
Roll size: 10m x 53cm
Repeat: unknown
Website: elitis.fr

Cole & Son
'Albany Damask Flock' (70/1002) from the Classix Exotic Flock Collection
Roll size: 10m x 52cm
Repeat: 53cm
Website: cole-and-son.com

Anya Larkin
'Artemis'
Roll size: by the metre x 101.5cm
Repeat: no repeat
Website: anyalarkin.com

Absolute Zero ° in collaboration with the Southbank Centre
'Net and Ball' in Black
Roll size: 10m x 52cm
Repeat: 53cm (straight match)
Website: southbankcentre.co.uk

Linda Florence
'Digital Flock Morphic Damask'
Roll size: by the metre x 53cm
Repeat: no repeat
Website: lindaflorence.co.uk

Maya Romanoff
'Mother of Pearl' in Fire Coral (MR.MP.22)
Roll size: minimum of 20 tiles
Repeat: 61cm x 30.5cm
Website: mayaromanoff.com

Harlequin
'Alta' (15867) from the Arkona Collection
Roll size: 10m x 52cm
Repeat: 52cm (straight match)
Website: harlequin.uk.com

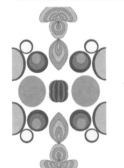

Madison & Grow
'Estella' in Berkshires on Parchment from the Pasadena Collection
Roll size: 4.5m x 68.6cm
Repeat: 48in (straight match)
Website: madisonandgrow.com

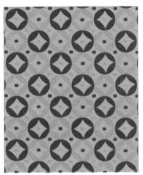

Sydney Albertini for Studio Printworks
'Byzantium' in Leander (SPW-W1047-01)
Roll size: 4.5m x 27in
Repeat: 68.5cm (straight match)
Website: studioprintworks.com

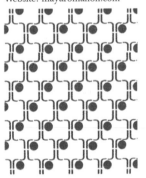

Given Campbell for Studio Printworks
'Pipes' in Hinson (SPW-W1046-06)
Roll size: 4.5m x 68.6cm
Repeat: 16.5cm (straight match)
Website: studioprintworks.com

Larsen
'Couture' in Jasper (L6061-07)
Roll size: 10m x 52cm
Repeat: 26cm
Website: larsenfabrics.com

Larsen
'Backdrop' in Peppercorn (L6063-10)
Roll size: 10m x 68.5cm
Repeat: no repeat
Website: larsenfabrics.com

Lambert
'Muna' in Black (80.006)
Roll size: made to order
Repeat: no repeat
Website: lambert-home.de

Jane Churchill at Colefax and Fowler
'Dorset' in Granite (J099W-03) from the Grovepark Collection
Roll size: 10m x 52cm
Repeat: 52cm
Website: janechurchill.com

Tres Tintas
'Ondas' (1967/4)
Roll size: 10m x 53cm
Repeat: 53cm
Website: trestintas.com

Romo
'Laurito Flock' in Ebony (W319/01)
Roll size: 10m x 52cm
Repeat: 41.8cm
Website: romo.com

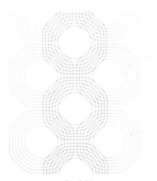

Extratapete GmbH
'Lui' 01 (Art-No 010603)
Roll size: 2.5m/3m/3.5m/4m x 46.5cm
Repeat: unknown
Website: extratapete.de

Extratapete GmbH
'Anna' (Art-No 010501)
Roll size: 2.5m/3m/3.5m/4m x 46.5cm
Repeat: 46.5cm (straight match)
Website: extratapete.de

Brian Yates
'Odeon'
Roll size: 8.5m x 70cm
Repeat: unknown
Website: brian-yates.co.uk

Basso & Brooke
for Graham & Brown
'Globe' in Cocoa (18342)
Roll size: 10m x 52cm
Repeat: 64cm
Website: grahambrown.com

Arte distributed by Brian Yates
'14203' from the Zenobia Collection
Roll size: 8.5m x 70cm
Repeat: 4.2cm
Website: brian-yates.co.uk

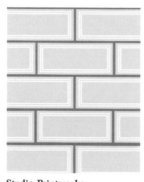

Studio Printworks
'Le Temple des Grec' in Bastille
(SPW-W1023-01)
Roll size: 4.5m x 68.6cm
Repeat: 58.4cm
Website: studioprintworks.com

Andrea Pößnicker distributed by Arte
'Lady Light' in Silver Metallic on Kohl
Black (3515) from the Pomp Collection
Roll size: 10m x 70cm
Repeat: 64cm
Website: pvanb.com

Andrea Pößnicker distributed by Arte
'Bricks' in Extra Virgin White Foam on
Flashy Neon Pink (2102)
Roll size: 10m x 53cm
Repeat: unknown
Website: pvanb.com

Maya Romanoff
'Komodo Vinyl Type II' in Willow
(MR.FV.01667)
Roll size: 27.4m x 137cm
Repeat: no repeat
Website: mayaromanoff.com

Nobilis
'Darnier Noyer Fonce' (PBM56)
Roll size: 6m x 91cm
Repeat: 10cm
Website: nobilis.fr

Omexco distributed by Brian Yates
'LAA101' from the Laguna Collection
Roll size: by the metre x 91cm
Repeat: 64cm
Website: brian-yates.co.uk

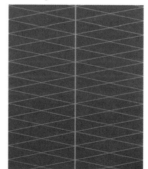

Natasha Marshall for Today Interiors
'Bridge' in Berry (GWP146) from the
Graphic Collection
Roll size: 10m x 53cm
Repeat: 5.4cm
Website: natashamarshall.co.uk

Natasha Marshall for Today Interiors
'Billow' in Twilight (ATW527)
Roll size: 10m x 53cm
Repeat: 68.5cm
Website: natashamarshall.co.uk

Dedar
'Alhambra' in Quesi Nero (D19008)
Roll size: 10m x 69cm
Repeat: 87cm
Website: dedar.it

Tres Tintas
'Espiga' (1962_1)
Roll size: 10m x 52cm
Repeat: 26cm
Website: trestintas.com

Tracy Kendall
'In the White Room'
Roll size: made to order, by the sq metre
Repeat: no repeat
Website: tracykendall.com

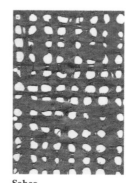

Sahco
'Oracle' (W019-03)
Roll size: by the metre x 122cm
Repeat: no repeat
Website: sahco-hesslein.com

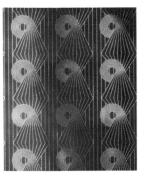

Erica Wakerly
'Mini Spiral' in Black/Silver
Roll size: 10m x 52cm
Repeat: 53cm
Website: printpattern.com

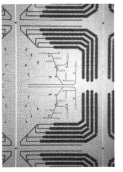

Neisha Crosland
'Donegal Palm' in Black Rose
(WV6DON-01)
Roll size: 10m x 52cm
Repeat: 76cm
Website: neishacrosland.com

Romo
'Tamino' in Fuchsia (W301/06)
Roll size: 10m x 52cm
Repeat: 15.3cm
Website: romo.com

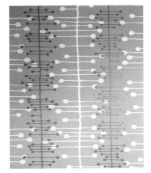

Miss Print
'Muscat' in Yellow (MISP1019)
Roll size: 10m x 52cm
Repeat: 52cm (straight match)
Website: missprint.co.uk

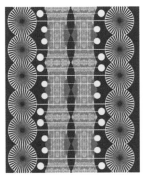

ATA Designs
'Trees' (ATAD1056)
Roll size: 10m x 52cm
Repeat: 31.42cm
Website: atadesigns.com

Hugh Dunford Wood
'Chevron' in Gatenby
Roll size: 10m x 56cm
Repeat: 20cm
Website: handmadewallpaper.co.uk

Andrew Hardiman for Kuboaa
'Allumette' in Broad Bean (KUAL01)
Roll size: 10m x 52cm
Repeat: 54cm (straight match)
Website: kuboaa.co.uk

Harlequin
'Contour' (60645) from the
Virtue Collection
Roll size: 10m x 52cm
Repeat: 26cm (straight match)
Website: harlequin.uk.com

Harlequin
'Vigour' (10312) in Silver on Black
from the Virtue Collection
Roll size: 10m x 52cm
Repeat: 52cm (straight match)
Website: harlequin.uk.com

Phillip Jeffries
'Spring' (3971) from the Seasons
Leaf Collection
Roll size: 7.3m x 91.5cm
Repeat: no repeat
Website: phillipjeffries.com

Cole & Son
'Haddon Hall' in White on Silver (CMW514)
from Classix Exotic Flock Collection
Roll size: 10m x 52cm
Repeat: 52.5cm
Website: cole-and-son.com

**Manuel Canovas
for Colefax and Fowler**
'Cassis' in Fuchsia (03042/04)
Roll size: 10m x 52cm
Repeat: 72cm
Website: manuelcanovas.com

Graham & Brown
'Buckingham' (12011) from the
Superfresco Paintable Collection
Roll size: 10m x 52cm
Repeat: 12.8cm
Website: grahambrown.com

Suzy Hoodless for Osborne & Little
'Foxglove' (W5805/01) from the
Hothouse Collection
Roll size: 10m x 52cm
Repeat: 76cm (half drop)
Website: osborneandlittle.com

Miss Print
'Fleur' in Lime (MISP1015)
Roll size: 10m x 52cm
Repeat: 52cm (half drop)
Website: missprint.co.uk

Harlequin
'Miya' from the Tamika Collection
Roll size: 10.5m x 68.6cm
Repeat: 76cm
Website: harlequin.uk.com

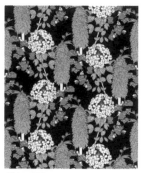

Abigail Borg
'Polka Polka'
Roll size: 10m x 54cm
Repeat: 23.79cm x 41.68cm
Website: abigailborg.co.uk

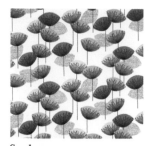

Sanderson
'Dandelion Clocks' in Chaffinch
(DOPWDA104)
Roll size: 10m x 52cm
Repeat: 64cm (half drop)
Website: sanderson-uk.com

Clarissa Hulse
'Dragonfly' in Pewter on Neon
Pink (2W-DRAGN-NE/P)
Roll size: 10m x 52cm
Repeat: 60cm (half drop)
Website: clarissahulse.com

Clarissa Hulse
'Reeds' in Turquoise on
Chocolate (1W-REEDS-CH-T)
Roll size: 10m x 52cm
Repeat: 53cm (half drop)
Website: clarissahulse.com

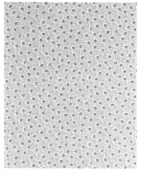

Designers Guild
'Primrose Hill' in Pink on
Turquoise (P492/04)
Roll size: 10m x 52cm
Repeat: 26cm (straight)
Website: designersguild.com

Designers Guild
'Maddalena' in Silver and Gold
on Black (P494/05)
Roll size: 10m x 52cm
Repeat: 64cm (straight)
Website: designersguild.com

Jill Malek
'Sleeping Briar Rose' in Noir (6-2)
Roll size: 4.5m x 68.6cm
Repeat: unknown
Website: jillmalek.com

**Florence Broadhurst
for Signature Prints**
'Tropical Floral' (FBW/FL32)
Roll size: 10m x 71cm
Repeat: 60.95cm
Website: signatureprints.com.au

Jocelyn Warner
'Treetops' in Silver Grey (JWP-1104)
Roll size: 10m x 68.5cm
Repeat: 72cm (straight match)
Website: jocelynwarner.com

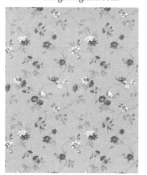

Nina Campbell for Osborne & Little
'Famille Rose' (NCW2070-08)
Roll size: 10m x 52cm
Repeat: 36cm
Website: osborneandlittle.com

Rachel Kelly
'Long Flower' in Coral and Stone
with Lustre
Roll size: 3m x 90cm
Repeat: no repeat
Website: interactivewallpaper.co.uk

Timorous Beasties
'Thistle' in Black on Ivory from the
Superwide Collection (SWP/THL/IVY/01)
Roll size: sold by the metre x 135cm
Repeat: 93cm
Website: timorousbeasties.com

Timorous Beasties
'Thistle' in Silver on Ivory from the
Superwide Collection (SWP/THL/IVY/02)
Roll size: 135cm wide, sold by the metre
Repeat: 93cm
Website: timorousbeasties.com

Henry Wilson for Osborne & Little
'Maharani' (W6022-01) from the
Sariskar Collection
Roll size: 10m x 52cm
Repeat: 102cm (quarter drop)
Website: osborneandlittle.com

Nancy Burgess for Studio Printworks
'Grand Pauline' in Golden Age
(SPW-W1044-08)
Roll size: 4.5m x 68.6cm
Repeat: 64.1cm
Website: studioprintworks.com

Fromental
'Chinon' in Cook (F009)
Roll size: made to order
Repeat: no repeat
Website: fromental.co.uk

Claire Coles
'Garden Scene 1'
Roll size: made to order in 3m drops
Repeat: no repeat
Website: clairecolesdesign.co.uk

Studio Printworks
'Fern' in Villa (SPW-1020-02)
Roll size: 4.5m x 68.6cm
Repeat: 54.6cm
Website: studioprintworks.com

**Manuel Canovas
at Colefax and Fowler**
'Clara' in Argent (03034/03)
Roll size: 10m x 52cm
Repeat: 52cm
Website: manuelcanovas.com

Watts of Westminster
'Percival' in Cardinal Graphite
(W0099-04)
Roll size: 10m x 62cm
Repeat: 183cm
Website: wattsofwestminster.com

Farrow & Ball
'St Antoine' in Blue on Grey (BP 9-51)
Roll size: 10m x 53cm
Repeat: 85cm
Website: farrow-ball.com

Lorca for Osborne & Little
'Cattleya' (MLW2066-03)
Roll size: 10m x 52cm
Repeat: 52cm (half drop)
Website: osborneandlittle.com

Lorca for Osborne & Little
'Ninfa' (MLW2060-06)
Roll size: 10m x 52cm
Repeat: 61cm (straight)
Website: osborneandlittle.com

Lorca for Osborne & Little
'Imperia' (MLW2061-01)
Roll size: 10m x 52cm
Repeat: 52cm (straight)
Website: osborneandlittle.com

Kirk Brummel
'Boca Chica – Positive' in Red on
White (BOCP-W1-166)
Roll size: 4.5m x 68.5cm
Repeat: unknown
Website: brunschwig.com

Billy McCarthy for Kirk Brummel
'Luxuriants Tracery' in Brown on Cream (LUXT-
W1-874) from In Search of Unicorns Collection
Roll size: 4.5m x 68.5cm
Repeat: 68.5cm
Website: brunschwig.com

Lim & Handtryck
'Höst' in Black on White (30111)
from the Funkis Collection
Roll size: 10m x 47cm
Repeat: 42cm
Website: limohandtryck.se

William Morris for Sanderson
'Fruit' in Coral Beige (WR8048/1)
Roll size: 10m x 52cm
Repeat: 54cm (straight)
Website: william-morris.co.uk

William Morris for Sanderson
'Golden Lily' in Pale Biscuit (WR8556/2)
Roll size: 10m x 52cm
Repeat: 46cm (straight)
Website: william-morris.co.uk

Tyler Hall
'First Bloom' in Snow Bud (8205/3)
Roll size: 4.5m x 68.6cm
Repeat: 91.4cm
Website: tyler-hall.com

Tyler Hall
'Kensington Gardens' (8206/4)
Roll size: 4.5m x 68.6cm
Repeat: 67.3cm
Website: tyler-hall.com

Tyler Hall
'Belgravia' (8204/1)
Roll size: 4.5m x 68.6cm
Repeat: 68.6cm
Website: tyler-hall.com

**Barbara Barry
for Kravet**
'In Bloom' in Chocolate (W3001-612)
Roll size: 10m x 52cm
Repeat: 70cm
Website: barbarabarry.com/kravet.com

The Silk Gallery Ltd
'Bouquet and Ribbon' in Blue Ribbon
and Coral Flower (SGWP-RIPEBL)
Roll size: 124cm wide, made to order
Repeat: 90cm
Website: thesilkgallery.com

Josef Frank for Svenskt Tenn
'Krysantemer' (809-52) in Yellow (816)
Roll size: 12.2m x 53cm
Repeat: 64cm
Website: svenskttenn.se

Emery & Cie
'Herbes Folles' (motif no. 1 on
background no. 77)
Roll size: made to order
Repeat: 85cm x 175cm
Website: emeryetcie.com

Miss Print
'Saplings' in Gold on Turquoise
(MISP1012)
Roll size: 10m x 52cm
Repeat: 13cm (quarter drop)
Website: missprint.co.uk

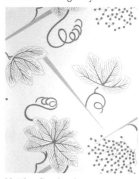

Neisha Crosland
'Currant Leaf' in Polar
(WV6CUR-02)
Roll size: 10m x 52cm
Repeat: 60cm
Website: neishacrosland.com

Neisha Crosland
'Firework Flowers' in Moss Pink
(WV6FIR-03)
Roll size: 10m x 68.5cm
Repeat: 61cm
Website: neishacrosland.com

Natasha Marshall for Today Interiors
'Bloom' in Gold (ATW549) from the
Atlantis Collection
Roll size: 10m x 53m
Repeat: 76cm
Website: natashamarshall.co.uk

Harlequin
'Iola' in Hot Pink (75644) from
the Arkona Collection
Roll size: 10m x 52cm
Repeat: 52cm
Website: harlequin.uk.com

The Little Greene Paint Co
'Great Ormond Street' in Verditure
(277GTVERDI)
Roll size: 10.5m x 52cm
Repeat: 61cm (half drop)
Website: thelittlegreene.com

Madison & Grow
'Eloise' in Leaves at Night
Roll size: 13.7m x 68.6cm
Repeat: 81.3cm
Website: madisonandgrow.com

Harlequin
'Florian' (60778) in Gold on Black
from the Arkona Collection
Roll size: 10m x 52cm
Repeat: 52cm
Website: harlequin.uk.com

Harlequin
'Kimiko' (35616) from the
Tamika Collection
Roll size: 10m x 52cm
Repeat: 46cm (straight)
Website: harlequin.uk.com

David Oliver
'Mazurka' in Chocolate con Gusto
(MAZU CHOC-326) from the
Orchestration Collection
Roll size: 10m x 52cm
Repeat: 7.57cm
Website: paintlibrary.co.uk

David Oliver
'Opium' in Sugar Pink
(OPIU SUGA-090) from the
Liberation Collection
Roll size: 10m x 52cm
Repeat: 53cm
Website: paintlibrary.co.uk

Ella Doran
'Sunlight Through Leaves'
Roll size: 10m x 53cm
Repeat: 30cm
Website: elladoran.co.uk

Deborah Bowness
'Filling Cabinets' from the
Salvage Collection
Roll size: 3.3m x 56cm
Repeat: no repeat
Website: deborahbowness.com

Lizzie Allen
'London Buses'
Roll size: 10m x 55cm or 3m panels
Repeat: no repeat
Website: lizzeallen.co.uk

Geoff McFetridge for Pottok
'All of Us'
Roll size: 4.5m x 63.5cm
Repeat: 81.3cm
Website: pottokprints.com

Geoff McFetridge for Pottok
'Little Whales'
Roll size: 4.5m x 63.5cm
Repeat: 81.3cm
Website: pottokprints.com

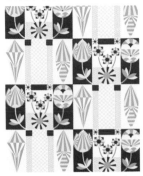

Geoff McFetridge for Pottok
'California Flowers'
Roll size: 4.5m x 63.5cm
Repeat: 81.3cm
Website: pottokprints.com

Inke Heiland
'Giraffe'
Roll size: 1.4m x 100cm
Repeat: no repeat
Website: inke.nl

Inke Heiland
'Vogeltjes'
Roll size: each bird measure 20cm x 25cm
Repeat: no repeat
Website: inke.nl

Charles Burger for Turnell & Gigon
'Ballon de Gonesse' in Jaune (2232-105)
Roll size: 10m x 53cm
Repeat: 60cm
Website: tandggroup.com

Timorous Beasties
'London Toile' in Green
(TB/LTOIL/4004/2)
Roll size: 10m x 52cm
Repeat: 92cm (quarter drop)
Website: timorousbeasties.com

Claire Coles
'Running Horses'
Roll size: made to order in 3m drops
Repeat: no repeat
Website: clairecolesdesign.co.uk

GP&J Baker
'Songbird' in Multi on Gold (BW 45004/1)
from the Emperor's Garden Collection
Roll size: 10m x 52cm
Repeat: 61cm
Website: gpjbaker.com

Judit Gueth
'Koi' in Chinoiserie (DWP0008)
Roll size: 9.1m x 45.7cm
Repeat: 23cm
Website: juditgueth.com

Judit Gueth
'Peacock' in Jade (DWP0001)
Roll size: 9.1m x 45.7cm
Repeat: 23cm
Website: juditgueth.com

Richard Neas for Brunschwig & Fils
'Bibliotheque' in Multi (14614-06)
Roll size: 4.5m x 68.6cm
Repeat: unknown
Website: brunschwig.com

ATA Designs
'City Series' (ATAD1019)
Roll size: 10m x 52cm
Repeat: 26cm
Website: atadesigns.com

Fromental
'Paradiso' in Ultramarine (C026)
Roll size: made to order
Repeat: no repeat
Website: fromental.co.uk

Schumacher
'Chiang Mai Dragon' in Alabaster
(SKU-5001063)
Roll size: 4.5m x 68.6cm
Repeat: 124.5cm (half drop)
Website: fschumacher.com

Pottok
'Apples Go Bananas'
Roll size: 4.5m x 63.5cm
Repeat: 81.3cm
Website: pottokprints.com

Hugh Dunford Wood
'Rousseau' in Fairground
Roll size: 10m x 56cm
Repeat: 20cm
Website: handmadewallpaper.co.uk

Absolute Zero °
'Tick-Tock' in Snow (AZDPT005)
Roll size: 10m x 52cm
Repeat: 53 (straight match)
Website: minimoderns.com

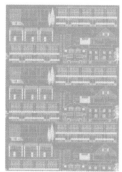

Absolute Zero °
'Do You Live in a Town?' in
Milk Chocolate (AZDPT001)
Roll size: 10m x 52cm
Repeat: 53cm (straight match)
Website: minimoderns.com

**Belynda Sharples
for The Art of Wallpaper**
'Chickens' (AOW-CHI-07)
Roll size: 10m x 52cm
Repeat: 53cm (straight match)
Website: theartofwallpaper.com

**Belynda Sharples
for The Art of Wallpaper**
'Countryside Toile' (AOW-COU-01)
Roll size: 10m x 52cm
Repeat: 53cm (half drop)
Website: theartofwallpaper.com

Lizzie Allen
'Changing the Guards at
Buckingham Palace' in Autum Gold
Roll size: 10m x 55cm
Repeat: 100cm
Website: lizzieallen.co.uk

Lizzie Allen
'London City Gents' in Autumn
Roll size: 10m x 55cm
Repeat: 60cm
Website: lizzieallen.co.uk

Lisa Bengtsson
'Familjen' (821-91)
Roll size: 10m x 53cm
Repeat: no repeat
Website: lisabengtsson.se

Paul Loebach for Studio Printworks
'Yee-Ha!' in Agent Orange
(SPW-W1043-09)
Roll size: 45.m x 68.6cm
Repeat: 33cm
Website: studioprintworks.com

Madison & Grow
'Erin' in Peacock on Shimmer
from the Pasadena Collection
Roll size: 4.5m x 68.6cm
Repeat: 3.6cm (straight match)
Website: madisonandgrow.com

Absolute Zero °
'Sitting Comfortably?' in Snow
(AZDPT007)
Roll size: 10m x 52cm
Repeat: 53cm (straight match)
Website: minimoderns.com

Celia Birtwell
'Beasties' in Red on Oyster (PW1258)
Roll size: 10m x 52cm
Repeat: 73cm
Website: celiabirtwell.com

Ornamenta
'Doves' in Tea Rose on Champagne (DOV8804)
from the Hand Printed Concept Collection
Roll size: 10m x 53cm
Repeat: 25cm
Website: ornamenta.com

Jill Malek
'Baby Elephant Walk' in Red Saffron (2-3)
Roll size: 10m x 52cm
Repeat: 53cm (straight match)
Website: jillmalek.com

**Florence Broadhurst for
Signature Prints**
'Egrets'
Roll size: 10m x 71cm
Repeat: 68.8cm
Website: signatureprints.com.au

Schumacher
'Aviary' in Multi on White
(SKU-2705511)
Roll size: 4.5m x 68.6cm
Repeat: 87.6cm
Website: fschumacher.com

Louise Body
'Erotica' in Black on White
Roll size: 10m x 52cm
Repeat: 76cm
Website: louisebodywallprint.com

Marthe Armitage
'Jungle Birds' in Black
Roll size: 10m x 58cm
Repeat: unknown
Website: hamiltonweston.com

Garin for Brian Lawrence
'Wallpaper Toile' (CTWPTBK)
Roll size: 10m x 58.5cm
Repeat: 59.6cm
Website: brianlawrence.net

Cath Kidston
'Boat' in White
Roll size: 10m x 52cm
Repeat: 61cm (half drop)
Website: cathkidston.co.uk

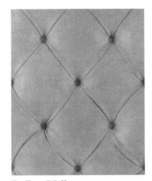

Endless Wallpaper
'Capitonné' in Green
Roll size: 1m or 3m x 46.5cm
Repeat: unknown
Website: endless-wallpaper.de

Mod Green Pod
'Butterfly Jubilee' (SKU02003011)
Roll size: 4.5m x 68.6cm
Repeat: 69.9cm x 68.6cm
Website: modgreenpod.com

Tracy Kendall
'Fork' from the Eat Collection
Roll size: 3.5m x 55cm
Repeat: no repeat
Website: tracykendall.com

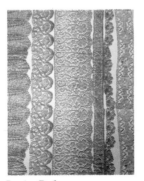

Louise Body
'Marney's Lace' in Charcoal
Roll size: 10m x 52cm
Repeat: 43cm
Website: louisebodywallprint.com

Ella Doran
'Stacks and Stripes'
Roll size: 10m x 53cm
Repeat: 30cm
Website: elladoran.co.uk

Ella Doran
'Sunlight Through Leaves'
Roll size: 10m x 53cm
Repeat: 30cm
Website: elladoran.co.uk

Marthe Armitage
'Manor House' in Dark Green
Roll size: 10m x 58cm
Repeat: unknown
Website: hamiltonweston.com

Endless Wallpaper
'Paradise Lila' (one of four panels)
Roll size: 2m x 46.5cm
Repeat: no repeat
Website: endless-wallpaper.de

de Gournay
'North American River Views'
handpainted wallpaper
Roll size: made to order
Repeat: no repeat
Website: degournay.com

Osborne & Little
'Best in Show' in Black on White (W5872-01)
from the Walk in Park Collection
Roll size: 10m x 52cm
Repeat: 21cm
Website: osborneandlittle.com

Cole & Son
'Woods' (69/12151) from the
Contemporary II Collection
Roll size: 10m x 52cm
Repeat: 72cm (halfdrop)
Website: cole-and-son.com

Dominic Crinson
'Londonscape' from the Murals Collection
Roll size: made to order
Repeat: no repeat
Website: crinson.com

Piero Fornasetti for Cole & Son
'Mediterranea' (77/5016) from
The Fornasetti Collection
Roll size: 10m x 52cm
Repeat: 76cm (half drop)
Website: cole-and-son.com

Fromental
'Mille Fleurs' in Indigo (E017)
Roll size: made to order
Repeat: no repeat
Website: fromental.co.uk

Fromental
'Nonsuch' in Unconscious Style on
Moongold Silk (UC001)
Roll size: made to order
Repeat: no repeat
Website: fromental.co.uk

Glossary of other wallpapers

For the wallpapers shown in the photographs of individual rooms, wherever possible I have listed the manufacturer and designer's name where applicable, the design name and/or design code, the measurements of the roll and the measurements of the repeat of the pattern and, of course, the website details. Every effort has been made to trace the copyright holders. The publisher apologises in advance for any unintentional omissions and would be pleased to insert the appropriate acknowledgement in any subsequent edition.

Page 11 i.e.Wallpaper, 'Vortex' (IEV-105-VORTEX) from the Silhouette Collection, 10m x 52cm, repeat 52cm, interiors-europe.co.uk

Page 15 Flavor Paper, 'Flower of Love' in Raspberry Sorbet, 4.57m x 68.5cm, repeat 142.25cm, flavorleague.com

Page 17 (top left) Cole & Son, 'Damask Flock' on Silver Foil (68/1006), from the Classix Exotic Flock Collection, 10m x 52cm, repeat 52.5cm, cole-and-son.com

Page 17 (bottom left) Cole & Son, 'Haddon Hall' on Silver Foil from Classix Exotic Flock Collection (CMW514), 10m x 52cm, repeat 52.5cm, cole-and-son.com

Page 17 (right) Cole & Son, 'Albany Damask Flock' (70/1002) from Classix Exotic Flock Collection, 10m x 52cm, repeat 53cm, cole-and-son.com

Page 18 (top left) Leather wall by Michela Curetti for Le Qr, made to order, leqr.it

Page 18 (bottom left) Tracy Kendall, 'Sequins', made to order, no repeat, tracykendall.com

Page 19 Hemingway Design for Graham & Brown, 'Concrete' (57144), 10m x 52cm, no repeat, grahambrown.com

Page 20 (top left) Maya Romanoff, 'Mother of Pearl Chevron', tile size 45.5cm x 45.5cm, no repeat, mayaromanoff.com

Page 20 (bottom left) Maya Romanoff, 'True Metals Trapezoid', tile size 30.5cm x 30.5cm, no repeat, mayaromanoff.com

Page 20 (right) Maya Romanoff, 'Precious Metals, 7.3m x 96.5cm, no repeat, mayaromanoff.com

Page 21 Deborah Bowness, 'Patterned Illusion' from the Illusions of Grandeur Collection, 3.3m x 54cm, no repeat, deborahbowness.com

Page 22 (bottom left) Hemingway Design for Graham & Brown, 'Red Brick' (57146), 10m x 52cm, repeat 53cm, grahambrown.com

Page 22 (right) Graham & Brown, 'Wood Effect', 10m x 52cm, repeat 53cm, grahambrown.com

Page 23 A.W.N. Pugin for Cole and Son, 'Gothic Lily', 10m x 52cm (minimum order 10 rolls), cole-and-son.com

Page 24: Osborne & Little, 'Minaret' (W551/04), 10m x 68.5cm, repeat 45.5cm, osborneandlittle.com

Page 25 (left) Ferm Living, 'Feather', 10m x 53cm, repeat 26.5cm, ferm-living.com

Page 27 (top left) Margaret Hildebrand for Rasch, 'Studie' (1949), roll size, repeat, rasch.de

Page 27 (bottom left) Heinrich Siepmann & Junger Westen for Rasch, original draft (c 1955) for wallpaper design, rasch.de

Page 27 (right): Skinkichi Tajiri for Rasch, 'Louisiana' (1955), roll size, repeat, rasch.de

Page 28 (top left) David Oliver, 'Liberation' in Buff from the Liberation Collection, 10m x 52cm, repeat 53cm, paintlibrary.co.uk

Page 28 (bottom left) David Oliver, 'Crystal' in Face Powder from the Debutantes Collection, 10m x 52cm, repeat 53cm, paintlibrary.co.uk

Page 28 (right) David Oliver, 'Liberation' in Vanilla from the Liberation Collection, 10m x 52cm, repeat 53cm, paintlibrary.co.uk

Page 29 Vintage 1970s wallpaper bought by the home owner in Italy

Page 30 (top) Jocelyn Warner, 'Kaleido' in Pink (JWP-802), 10m x 52cm, repeat 20.53cm, jocelynwarner.com

Page 31 (main) Graham & Brown, 'Vogue' (18067) from the Superfresco Collection, 10m x 50cm, repeat 64cm, grahambrown.com

Page 31 (bottom left) Graham & Brown, from the Superfresco Collection, 10m x 50cm, repeat 64cm, grahambrown.com

Page 81 Rapture and Wright, 'Waimea' in Clove, 10m x 52cm, repeat 63cm, raptureandwright.co.uk

Page 86 (centre) Eijffinger, Flo Collection, eijffinger.nl

Page 87 Rapture and Wright, 'Waimea' in Clove, 10m x 52cm, repeat 63cm, raptureandwright.co.uk

Page 88 (top left) Josef Frank for Svenskt Tenn, 'Vårklockor' in White, 10m x 53cm, repeat 56cm, svenskttenn.se

Page 88 (bottom left) Josef Frank for Svenskt Tenn, 'Vårklockor' in Black, 10m x 53cm, repeat 56cm, svenskttenn.se

Page 88 (top right) Josef Frank for Svenskt Tenn, 'Krysantemer' in Red, 12.2m x 53cm, repeat 64cm, svenskttenn.se

Page 89 (top, in panel) Designers Guild, 'Imperial Flower' in Black and White, 10m x 52cm, repeat 60cm, designersguild.com

Page 89 (bottom, under dado) Designers Guild, 'Cloisonne' in Black and White, 10m x 52cm, repeat 91cm, designersguild.com

Page 91 (background) Designers Guild, 'Amalienborg' in Amethyst, 10m x 52cm, repeat 69cm, designersguild.com

Page 91 (foreground) Designers Guild, 'Marionlyst' in Gold, 10m x 52cm, repeat 64cm, designersguild.com

Page 93 (top left) Sanderson, from the Triad Collection, sandersonfabrics.com

Page 93 (right) Sanderson, 'Ivy' from the Triad Collection, sandersonfabrics.com

Page 95 (foreground) Designers Guild, 'Corazon' in Schiaparelli, 10m x 52cm, repeat 53cm, designersguild.com

Page 96 (left) Cole & Son, 'Woods' (69/12150) from the Contemporary II Collection, 10m x 52cm, repeat 72cm, cole-and-son.com

Page 97 (top left) Neisha Crosland, 'Flamenco' in Pearl Grey (WV5FLA02) from the Papers Five Collection, 10m x 68.5cm, repeat 48cm, neishacrosland.com

Page 97 (centre left) Neisha Crosland, 'Bird Tree' in Canary Yellow from the Papers Three Collection, 10m x 52cm, repeat 60cm, neishacrosland.com

Page 97 (bottom left) Neisha Crosland, 'Currant Leaf' in Cedar Green (WV6CUR-01) from the Papers Six Collection, 10m x 52cm, repeat 60cm, neishacrosland.com

Page 97 (centre left) Neisha Crosland, 'Bird Tree' in Cockatoo Red from the Papers Three Collection, 10m x 52cm, repeat 60cm, neishacrosland.com

Page 98 (top left) Florence Broadhurst, 'Egrets' in Keyline Oriental Blue & Smalt (FBW/BO28) from the Blueprints Collection, 10m x 71cm, repeat 67.5cm, signatureprints.com.au

Page 98 (centre left) Florence Broadhurst, 'Japanese Floral' in Stormy Seas (FBW/CO07), 10m x 61cm, repeat 61cm, signatureprints.com.au

Page 98 (bottom left) Florence Broadhurst, 'Floral 100' in Distant Cloud (FBW/BO89), 10m x 71cm, repeat 58.9cm, signatureprints.com.au

Page 98 (right) Florence Broadhurst, 'Floral 300' in Chalk Blue (FBW/BO93), 10m x 71cm, repeat 60.9cm, signatureprints.com.au

Page 100 Cole & Son, 'Rococo Leopard' (72/8031) from the Patina Collection, 10m x 52cm, repeat 72cm, cole-and-son.com

Page 101 Cole & Son, 'Rococo Leopard' (72/8031) from the Patina Collection, 10m x 52cm, repeat 72cm, cole-and-son.com

Page 102 Timorous Beasties, 'Thistle' in Black on Ivory (SWP/THL/IVY/01), sold by the metre x 135cm, repeat 93cm, timorousbeasties.com

Page 104 (top left) Designers Guild, 'Margot' in Acacia (P503/03/C), 10m x 52cm, repeat 80cm, designersguild.com

Page 104 (bottom left) Designers Guild, 'Eldridge', 10m x 52cm, repeat 64cm, designersguild.com

Page 104 (right) Designers Guild, 'Margot' in Acacia (P503/03/C), 10m x 52cm, repeat 80cm, designersguild.com

Page 105 (top left) Ferm Living, 'Family Tree' (127), 10m x 53cm, repeat 53cm, ferm-living.com

Page 105 (bottom left) Ferm Living, 'Family Tree' (126), 10m x 53cm, repeat 53cm, ferm-living.com

Page 105 (right) Ferm Living, 'Ribbed' (118), 10m x 53cm, repeat 53cm, ferm-living.com

Page 106 (left) Kirk Brummel for Brunschwig & Fils, 'Luxuriants on Paper'in grape/chartreuse/pink on white (LUXU-W7-761), 4.5m x 68.6cm, repeat 68.6cm, brunschwig.com

Page 106 (right) Kirk Brummel for Brunschwig & Fils, 'Shawnee', brunschwig.com

Page 107 Cole & Son, 'Lily' (69/3113) from the Contemporary II Collection, 10m x 52cm, repeat 76cm, cole-and-son.com

Page 108 Osborne & Little, 'Edo' (W5226/05) from the Sakura Collection, 10m x 52cm, repeat 72cm, osborneandlittle.com

Page 109 Farrow & Ball, 'Saint Antoine' (BP910), 10m x 53cm, repeat 85cm, farrow-ball.com

Page 110 (top) Schumacher, 'Trelliage Imperial Trellis' (2707212), 12.3m x 68.8cm, repeat 35.6cm, fschumacher.com

Page 111 Pomme Jeune by Mauny from Zuber et Cie, zuber.fr

Page 164 Fromental, 'Embroidered Millefleurs' in Odyssey, made to order, no repeat, fromental.com

Page 165 Deborah Bowness, 'Genuine Fake Bookshelf', 3.3m x 54/56cm, no repeat, deborahbowness.com

Page 166 (top left) Dorkenwald-Spitzer, 'Sacco' from the Wall Furniture Collection, 1.8m x 2.2m, no repeat, dorkenwald-spitzer.com

Page 166 (centre) Dorkenwald-Spitzer, '85 Lamps' from the Wall Furniture Collection, 1.8m x 2.2m, no repeat, dorkenwald-spitzer.com

Page 166 (bottom) Dorkenwald-Spitzer, 'LC2' from the Wall Furniture Collection, 1.8m x 2.2m, no repeat, dorkenwald-spitzer.com

Page 167 (**top left**) Deborah Bowness, 'Rose Dress' from the Wallpaper Frocks Collection, 3.3m x 56cm, no repeat, deborahbowness.com

Page 167 (**centre left**) Tracy Kendall, 'Open Feather' and 'Slim Feather', 2.15m x 55cm, no repeat, tracykendall.com

Page 167 (**right**) Deborah Bowness, 'Kim's Lamp' from the Standard Lamp Wallpaper Collection, 1.8m x 52cm, no repeat, deborahbowness.com

Page 168 (**top left**) Roger Nicholson for Lightbown and Aspinall, 'Hopscotch' (1955)

Page 168 (**bottom left**) Roger Nicholson for Lightbown and Aspinall, 'Locomotion' (1958)

Page 168 (**right**) Roger Nicholson for Lightbown and Aspinall, 'Hopscotch' (1955)

Page 169 Tracy Kendall, 'Plates' from the Stack Collection, made to order, by the metre x 46.5cm, no repeat, tracykendall.com

Page 170 Gracie Studio, hand-painted Chinese Scenic panel, made to order, graciestudio.com

Page 171 (**top**) Surface View, 'Lost Classics Lady of the Orient' mural from the Land of Lost Content Collection, surfaceview.co.uk

Page 171 (**bottom left**) 'LC2' from the Wall Furniture collection by Dorkenwald-Spitzer, 1.8m x 220cm, no repeat, dorkenwald-spitzer.com

Page 171 (**bottom right**) David Lee at Photographic Interiors, 'Photographic Frieze', www.photographicinteriors.com

Page 172 (**main**) Martine Aballe, bespoke paper, made to order, no repeat.

Page 173 (**left**) Surface View, 'Bespoke Vinyl Wall', no repeat, surfaceview.co.uk

Page 175 E.W. Moore, 'Code C810' from Wallposters Collection, 2.64m x 3.96m, no repeat, ewmoore.com

Page 176 (**top left**) Fromental, 'Floribunda' in Blue Light, made to order, no repeat, fromental.co.uk

Page 176 (**bottom left**) Fromental, 'Paradiso' in Kelly, made to order, no repeat, fromental.co.uk

Page 176 (**right**) Fromental, 'Paradiso' in Mustard Grass, made to order, no repeat, fromental.co.uk

Page 177 Cole & Son, 'Flamingos' (66/6044), 10m x 52cm, repeat 72cm, cole-and-son.com

Page 178 De Gournay, 'North American River View', made to order, no repeat, degournay.com

Page 179 Zuber et Cie, 'Hindoustan', panel size 3.9m x 67cm, made to order, no repeat, zuber.fr

Page 180 Fromental, 'Paradiso' in Mustard Grass, made to order, no repeat, fromental.co.uk

Page 181 (**top left**) Gracie Studio, 'SY-233', panel size 3m x 91.5cm or made to order, no repeat, graciestudio.com

Page 181 (**bottom left**): Gracie Studio, 'SY-223', panel size 3m x 91.5cm or made to order, no repeat, graciestudio.com

Page 181 (**right**) Gracie Studio, 'SY-232', panel size 3m x 91.5cm or made to order, no repeat, graciestudio.com

Page 182 (**top left**) Celia Birtwell, 'Beasties' in Red on Oyster (PW1258), 10m x 52cm, repeat 73cm, celiabirtwell.com

Page 182 (**bottom left and right**) Celia Birtwell, 'Jacobean at Night' (PW257), 10m x 52cm, repeat 61cm, celiabirtwell.com

Page 183 (**left**) Les Toiles Villageoise

Index

Picture credits

Special photography © Beth Evans pages 100–101, 107, 164, 177 and 180.

The publisher would like to thank the following photographers, agencies and companies for their kind permission to reproduce the photographs in this book:

11 Sean Myers/Media10 Images; **14** Ray Main/Mainstream Images; **15** Giulio Oriani/Vega Mg; **16** Ed Reeve/Red Cover; **17** courtesy of Cole & Son Ltd; **18 above** Jonas von der Hude/ Schoener Whonen/Camera Press; **18 below left** Beth Evans (Tracy Kendall); **18 below right** Hotze Eisma/Taverne Agency; **19** Rachael Smith/courtesy of Graham & Brown; **20** courtesy of Maya Romanoff; **21** Hufvudsta Gård Konferens AB; **22 above left** courtesy of Fromental; **22 below left** courtesy of Graham & Brown; **22 right** Mel Yates/Living Etc/ IPC+ Syndication; **23** courtesy of Cole & Son; **24** Bieke Claessens/Red Cover; **25 left** Bjarni B. Jacobsen (Stylist: Anette Eckmann)/Pure Public; **25 right** Juan Hitters (Architect, Interior and Furniture designer: Paula Lavarello)/Sur Press Agency; **26 left** Christophe Dugied/Madame Figaro/Camera Press; **26 right** Bjarni B. Jacobsen (Stylist: Anette Eckmann)/ Pure Public; **27** courtesy of Rasch; **28** courtesy of Paint and Paper Library; **29** A. Ianniello/Studiopep; **30 above** Edina van der Wyck/Media 10 Images; **30 below** Richard Powers (Designer: Nathan Egan Interiors); **31** courtesy of Graham & Brown; **81** Claudia Dulak/Media 10 Images; **84** Richard Powers (Architect: Scott Weston Architecture Design); **85** Francois Halard/Trish South Management/Trunk Archive; **86 above** Ewout Huibers (Stylist: Chrissie Cremers); **86 below** Christopher Drake/Red Cover; **87** Beth Evans (Owner: Nikki Tibbles of Wild at Heart Interiors); **88** courtesy of Svenskt Tenn; **89** courtesy of Designers Guild; **90** Nathalie Krag/ Taverne Agency; **91** Mel Yates/Living Etc/IPC+ Syndication; **92** Lorenzo Nencioni/Vega Mg; **94** above Alexander van Berge/Taverne Agency; **93** courtesy of Sanderson; **94** below Chris Tubbs/Red Cover; **95** Denise Bonenti (Stylist: Federica Foltran)/Vega Mg; **96 left** Ngoc Minh Ngo/Taverne Agency;

96 right Ray Main/Mainstream Images; **97 below left** Jan Baldwin at Pearson Lyle Management; **98** courtesy of Signature Prints; **99 above** Jan Baldwin/Narratives; **99 below** John Dummer/Taverne Agency; **102** Paul Raeside/Mainstream Images; **103** Bjarni B. Jacobsen (Stylist: Anette Eckmann)/Pure Public; **104** courtesy of Designers Guild; **105** courtesy of Ferm Living; **108 above** Pernille Kaalund (Stylist: Louise Kamman Riising)/Pure Public; **108 below** Jan Baldwin/ Narratives; **109** M. Bayle/Philippe Garcia/MCM/Camera Press; **110 above** Francois Halard/Trish South Management/ Trunk Archive; **110 below** Chris Tubbs (Designer: Sera Hersham-Loftus)/Red Cover; **111** Andreas von Einsiedel (Designer: Philip Hooper); **161** Ray Main/Mainstream Images (Designer: Jo Warman); **165** Polly Eltes/Abigail Ahern/Narratives; **166 above right** Tom Arban; **166 below left and right** courtesy of Dorkenwald-Spitzer; **167 above left** Liselotte Plenov/House of Pictures; **167 below left** M. Bayle/Philippe Garcia/MCM/ Camera Press; **167 right** courtesy of Deborah Bowness; **168** Museum of Domestic Design & Architecture, Middlesex University; **169** Beth Evans (Tracy Kendall); **170** Richard Powers (Designer: Kevin Haley); **171 above** Beth Evans (Interior Design: Gerardine & Wayne Hemingway of Hemingway Design); **171 below left** courtesy of Dorkenwald-Spitzer; **171 below right** Edina van der Wyck/Media 10 Images; **172 above** Yannick Labrousse/MCM/Camera Press (www.hotel-particulier-montmarte.com); **172 below** Chris Tubbs; **173 left** Mel Yates/Living Etc/IPC+ Syndication; **173 right** Richard Powers (Artist: Rodrigo Bueno); **174** Hotze Eisma/Taverne Agency; **175** Paul Massey/Living Etc/IPC+ Syndication; **176** courtesy of Fromental; **178** courtesy of de Gournay; **179** courtesy of Zuber et Cie; **181** courtesy of Gracie; **182** Beth Evans for Celia Birtwell Ltd; **183 left** Andreas von Einsiedel (Deisgner: Kenyon Kramer); **183 right** Richard Powers (Designer: Jacob Blom).

Every effort has been made to trace the copyright holders. We apologise in advance for any unintentional omissions and would be pleased to insert the appropriate acknowledgement in any subsequent edition.

Project Director: **Anne Furniss**
Project Editor: **Lisa Pendreigh**
Art Director: **Helen Lewis**
Designer: **Lucy Gowans**
Picture Researcher: **Liz Boyd**
Illustrator: **Bridget Bodoano**
Design Assistant: **Katherine Cordwell**
Production Director: **Vincent Smith**
Production Controller: **Aysun Hughes**

First published in 2009 by
Quadrille Publishing Limited
Alhambra House
27–31 Charing Cross Road
London WC2H 0LS
www.quadrille.co.uk

Reprinted in 2010
10 9 8 7 6 5 4 3 2

British Library Cataloguing-in-Publication Data
A catalogue record for this book is available from the British Library.

ISBN 978 184400 741 7

Printed in China

This book has been printed in Hexachrome®, an advanced printing process that uses six component
colours rather than the conventional four. While Heachrome® offers over 3,000 controllable colours,
there are still some limitations and variations within the printing process. As a result, it is
impossible to guarantee the fidelity of the colours reproduced. It is important to note that
different batches of wallpaper from any manufacturer will vary minutely in
colour. When buying wallpaper, always check the
batch numbers on the roll and buy from the
same batch whenever possible.